高职高专英语专业精品教材

U0062773

实用英语简捷语法

朱晓博　编著

北京理工大学出版社
BEIJING INSTITUTE OF TECHNOLOGY PRESS

图书在版编目（CIP）数据

实用英语简捷语法 / 朱晓博编著. — 北京：北京
理工大学出版社，2022.12（2023.1重印）
　ISBN 978-7-5763-1949-1

　Ⅰ.①实… 　Ⅱ.①朱… 　Ⅲ.①英语—语法—高等职业
教育—教材 　Ⅳ.①H319.35

　中国版本图书馆CIP数据核字（2022）第243715号

出版发行 / 北京理工大学出版社有限责任公司

社　　　址 / 北京市海淀区中关村南大街 5 号
邮　　　编 / 100081
电　　　话 /（010）68914775（总编室）
　　　　　　（010）82562903（教材售后服务热线）
　　　　　　（010）68944723（其他图书服务热线）
网　　　址 / http://www.bitpress.com.cn
经　　　销 / 全国各地新华书店
印　　　刷 / 三河市天利华印刷装订有限公司
开　　　本 / 787 毫米 × 1092 毫米　1/16
印　　　张 / 15.75　　　　　　　　　　　　　　　　责任编辑 / 时京京
字　　　数 / 315 千字　　　　　　　　　　　　　　　文案编辑 / 时京京
版　　　次 / 2022 年 12 月第 1 版　2023 年 1 月第 2 次印刷　　责任校对 / 刘亚男
定　　　价 / 45.00 元　　　　　　　　　　　　　　　责任印制 / 施胜娟

前言
Preface

英语语法是英语学习者学好英语的必备基础。《实用英语简捷语法》共分为三大模块：词的基本用法、句子与特殊结构、语法的综合运用。在词的基本用法模块，系统介绍了名词，代词，冠词，数词，介词，形容词，副词，动词和动词短语，情态动词，动词的时态、语态、语气和非谓语动词；在句子与特殊结构模块，全面介绍了简单句和并列句、名词性从句、定语从句、状语从句、主谓一致和一些特殊句式；在语法的综合运用模块，主要介绍了各项语法规则在词汇、完形填空、阅读理解和翻译题型中的具体应用。

本书的编写遵循以下几点原则：

一、定位具体，适用性强

本书定位明确，使用范围广。主要适用于高职高专英语专业学生、高职高专非英语专业学生、有专升本需求的学生，以及社会各界英语爱好者。

二、结构清晰，内容简捷

本书结构清晰，章节和内容编排科学合理，简明扼要，通俗易懂。

三、资源完整，配套齐全

本书内容除英语语法规则外，还提供了拓展材料，包括：习题、参考答案、常见短语、双语热词、教学课件等，方便教师授课和学生自学。

在编写过中，编者参考了大量相关书籍、报刊和网络材料，借鉴了一些宝贵的观点。在此予以说明并向有关作者致以真挚的谢意。

由于编者的经验和水平有限，难免存在不足之处，敬请专家和广大读者批评指正。

编者

2022 年 9 月

目录
Contents

第一章　词的基本用法

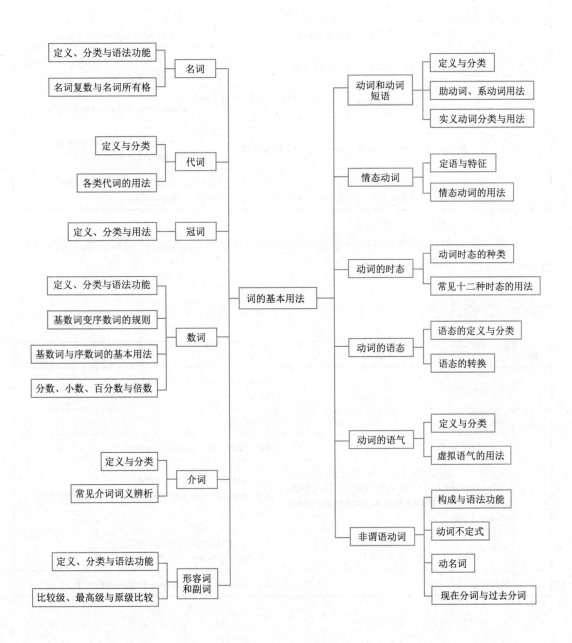

第一节 名词

一、名词的定义和分类

（1）定义：表示人或事物以及抽象概念名称的词。

（2）分类：按照意义可分为专有名词和普通名词。

分类名称		特征	例词
普通名词	个体名词	表示单个人或事物的名称	city, school, teacher, boy…
	集体名词	表示多个人或事物的总称	furniture, police, audience, youth, staff, army, cattle…
	物质名词	表示物质的名称，包括：材料、液体、气体、食物、饮料等的名词	gold, ink, oxygen, sand, juice…
	抽象名词	表示人或物的品质、状态等抽象概念	progress, anger, happiness, knowledge, hatred…
专有名词		特指人或事物的名称，首字母必须大写，包括：人名、地名、书名、月份、星期、组织机构名称等	the Great Wall, Steve Jobs, September…

个体名词和集体名词可以用数字来计算，称为可数名词；物质名词和抽象名词一般无法用数字计算，称为不可数名词。

二、名词的语法功能

序号	语法功能	例句
1	作主语、宾语	The boy broke his leg last week. He lost the game.
2	作表语	She is a liar.
3	作宾（主）语补足语	We consider him a good teacher.
4	作定语：常用单数形式，如：evening paper, night club, heart trouble, science fiction 等，特定短语中用复数形式，如：sports car, careers guidance, savings bank 等。	The winter vacation is coming. In America, people pay sales tax on many items they buy.
5	作状语	He stayed there (for) five days. The meeting lasted (for) hours.
6	作同位语	He, a famous writer, is easy to get along with.

三、名词复数的表达

（一）可数名词复数的变化规则

1. 规则变化

规则		例词	
一般情况下加 s		cake–cakes tourist–tourists	bird–birds
以 s, x, ch, sh 结尾的加 es		bus–buses watch–watches	box–boxes brush–brushes
以辅音字母 +o 结尾	加 es	Negro–Negroes potato–potatoes	hero–heroes tomato–tomatoes
	加 s	hippo–hippos photo–photos	piano–pianos kilo–kilos
	两者皆可	zero–zeros/zeroes volcano–volcanos/volcanoes	mango–mangos/mangoes
以元音字母 +o 结尾	加 s	radio–radios bamboo–bamboos	zoo–zoos
以辅音字母 +y 结尾	变 y 为 i 加 es	candy–candies, strawberry–strawberries	
以 f 或 fe 结尾	变 f、fe 为 v 加 es	knife–knives thief–thieves life–lives wife–wives	leaf–leaves loaf–loaves shelf–shelves wol–wolves
	直接加 s	roof–roofs proof–proofs	belief–beliefs chief–chiefs

2. 不规则变化

单复数同形	fish–fish, sheep–sheep, deer–deer, means–means
特殊形式	man–men woman–women postman–postmen foot–feet tooth–teeth mouse–mice child–children goose–geese crisis–crises analysis–analyses basis–bases datum–data medium–media bacterium–bacteria phenomenon–phenomena

> ➤ "……国人" 变复数

记忆小窍门：中日不变英法变，其他"s"加后面.

Chinese → Chinese　　　　　　Japanese → Japanese

Englishman → Englishmen	Frenchman → Frenchmen
American → Americans	Italian → Italians
German → Germans	Korean → Koreans

（二）复合名词的复数

1	"名词 + 名词"构成的复合名词，将第二个名词变成复数	traffic light → traffic lights blood type → blood types	
2	"名词 + 介词 + 名词"构成的复合名词，将第一个名词变成复数	son-in-law → sons-in-law editor-in-chief → editors-in-chief	
3	"名词以外的词类 + 名词"构成的复合名词，将名词变成复数	greenhouse → greenhouses looker-on → lookers-on	reading-room → reading-rooms passer-by → passers-by
4	名词以外的词类构成的复合名词，通常把最后一个词变成复数	go-between → go-betweens grown-up → grown-ups	
5	由 man 或 woman 构成的复合名词，两个词都变成复数	man-servant → men-servants woman doctor → women doctors	

（三）只有复数形式的名词

1	由两部分组成的东西的名词	scissors	trousers	compasses	pants
		shorts	glasses	scales	spectacles
2	一些词尾为 -ings 的名词	savings	findings	earnings	belongings	surroundings
3	其他以复数形式出现的名词：有些名词在表示某个特定的意义时，只有复数形式，表示复数的意义	remains 残余、残留物 arms 武器 looks 外貌 funds 基金 regards 问候 brains 智力		outskirts 郊区 clothes 衣服 goods 商品、货品 manners 礼貌、礼节 customs 海关 papers 论文、文件、报纸	

（四）不可数名词数的表达

一般来说，不可数名词只有单数形式，没有复数形式，但可以通过使用单位词的方式进行表达。

a piece/sheet of paper → two pieces/sheets of paper

a loaf/piece of bread → two loaves/pieces of bread

a bar of chocolate/gold → three bars of chocolate/gold

a bottle of beer/juice → three bottles of beer/juice

a tin of beer → four tins of beer

a basket of fruit → ten baskets of fruit

a drop of water	→	five drops of water
a kilo of sugar	→	ten kilos of sugar
a piece of news/advice	→	several pieces of news/advice

四、名词所有格

（一）'s 所有格的变化规则

序号	变化规则	例词
1	一般情况下加 's	Peter's　　　my mother's
2	以 s 结尾的人名，加 ' 或 's	Hans　→　Hans'/Hans's
3	以 s 结尾的复数名词，加 '	students'　　teachers'
4	不以 s 结尾的复数名词，加 's	men's　　children's
5	复合名词或名词短语的所有格是在最后一个词尾加 's 构成的	her brother–in–law's car the Government of China's policy go–betweens' arrangements somebody else's problem

（二）'s 所有格的用法

序号	用法	例词／句
1	表示所有关系、所属关系、动作执行者及动作承受者等意义。后面可加名词，也可以单独使用，作主语或表语	the dog's bark the cat's paw —Whose dress is this? —This is Mary's dress.(This is Mary's.)
2	有些表示时间、距离、度量、价值、自然现象、国家、城镇等无生命的名词，也可以加 's 构成所有格	an hour's ride the government's policy thirteen ton's weight a dollar's worth China's population five hundred metres' distance London's weather the sun's energy
3	and 连接两个名词，如果表示共同拥有，后面的名词加 's；如果表示分别拥有，两个名词分别加 's	Lucy and Lily's room　　Lucy's and Lily's rooms
4	表示店铺、住所等	I'll spend the weekend at my uncle's. When I got to the doctor's, there were already many people there. The dentist's is open until midnight. He is at the barber's/baker's/tailor's/butcher's.

（三）of 所有格

序号	用法	例词/句
1	用于无生命的名词	the cover of a magazine the color of her dress the leg of the table the cost of living
2	名词或代词后有后置定语时，要用 of 所有格	the name of the girl standing at the gate the book of the boy behind the door
3	"the+ 形容词"表示"一类人或物"的名词后要用 of 所有格	the living condition of the unemployed the education of the young
4	表示人、动物、时间、机构、组织等名词后往往可以用 of 所有格代替特指的名词所有格	Dickens's works = the works of Dickens the government's plan = the plan of the government

（四）双重所有格："of+…'s"双重所有格；of+ 名词性物主代词

如果被修饰的名词前有不定冠词、数词、不定限定词等，其后的定语要用双重所有格形式，of 后面只能接特指人的名词所有格或名词性物主代词。由双重所有格修饰的名词与指示限定词 this, that 连用时，表示爱憎、褒贬等感情色彩。

a friend of my brother's   another mistake of yours

some bad habits of theirs'   two daughters of Mr Smith's

this lovely child of your sister's   that long face of John's

---

> ➤ **知识点拓展**

1. people/peoples

（1）The cinema can hold more than 300 people.

（2）China consists of 56 peoples.

2. work/works

（1）We were very busy yesterday, because we had a lot of work to do.

（2）Shakespear's works have already been translated into Chinese.

3. wood/woods

（1）Their dishes were made of wood.

（2）Let's have a walk in the woods.

4. room/rooms

（1）There ins't enough room for all the furniture.

（2）I had all the rooms cleaned and aired.

5. time/times

（1）It took me two hours to finish the task.

（2）Johnny has changed his image to fit the times.

6. sand/sands

（1）She got some sand in her eye.

（2）The children are playing on the sands.

7. damage/damages

（1）The cost of the damage to the city was estimated at $ 18 million.

（2）The judge awarded him $1,000 as damages.

8. paper/papers

（1）He folded the paper carefully.

（2）The papers in maths and English are very difficult.

9. spectacle/spectacles

（1）It was a spectacle not to be missed.

（2）He looked at me over the tops of his spectacles.

10. experience/experiences

（1）How much experience do you have in teaching English?

（2）We had several terrible experiences during our trip.

专项练习题

一、用所给单词的适当形式填空

1. I can not see the blackboard clearly. I need to wear ＿＿（glass）.

2. The ＿＿（light）was not very good so it was difficult to read.

3. Nowadays, we have many ＿＿（woman）drivers.

4. This isn't my key; it must be someone ＿＿（else）.

5. The lady in blue is a friend of ＿＿（Alice mother）.

6. Mary's handwriting is better than any other＿＿（student）in her class.

7. My school is five ＿＿（minute）walk from here.

8. There are many ＿＿（German）living in Shenyang.

9. The men you just saw here are my ＿＿（brother-in-law）.

10. ＿＿（bamboo）are not real trees. In fact, they are grass.

11. Thousands of people lost their ＿＿＿（life）in the war.

12. Herbs have been used to make drinks for ＿＿＿（century）.

13. David is a friend of my ＿＿＿（brother）. We often play basketball together.\

14. Do you still have ＿＿＿（yesterday）newspaper?

15. They have bought a lot of ＿＿＿（furniture）for their new house.

二、单项选择题

1. ＿＿＿ important to everybody.

    A. Honesty being   B. The Honesty is

    C. A honesty is   D. Honesty is

2. China has ＿＿＿ of more than 1.4 billion.

    A. much population   B. the population

    C. a little population   D. a population

3. We were very busy yesterday, because we had ＿＿＿ to do.

    A. much work   B. many work

    C. much job   D. a lot of job

4. ——Excuse me, how can I get to the nearest bus stop?

    ——Go down this road. It's about ＿＿＿ walk.

    A. five minute's   B. five minutes'

    C. five–minutes   D. five minute

5. ——How far is it from Tianjin to Changsha?

    ——It is a ＿＿＿ flight.

    A. 2–hour–long   B. 2–hours–long

    C. 2 hours' long   D. 2 hour long

6. Mr. Black has a strong ＿＿＿ of duty.

    A. feeling   B. idea

    C. thought   D. sense

7. He has poor ＿＿＿, so he can't see the words on the blackboard clearly.

    A. smell   B. taste

    C. hearing   D. eyesight

8. We called at ＿＿＿ yesterday.

    A. my uncle   B. my uncle's

    C. a friend of my uncle   D. my uncles'

9. Peter regards Nanjing as his second ____ because he has lived here for ten years.

    A. family   B. house

    C. home   D. room

10. ——Could you please tell me something about the two ____?

    ——____. They are exchange students of No.1 Middle School.

    A.Frenchmen; Yes, please   B. Frenchmans; Come on

    C. German; Not at all   D. Germans; All right

11. ——Mrs. Wang was sent to teach English in a poor mountain village last year.

    ——She said she would never forget some pleasant ____ while working there.

    A. experiments   B. expressions

    C. experiences   D. excitement

12. Stop making so much ____. The children are sleeping.

    A. voice   B. noise

    C. sound   D. talk

13. ____ heavy in big cities.

    A. The traffic are   B. The traffic is

    C. The traffics are   D. The traffics is

14. ——You are always full of ____. Can you tell me the secret?

    ——Taking plenty of exercises every day.

    A. strength   B. energy

    C. force   D. power

15. It's common ____ that the Japanese eat Sushi.

    A. information   B. knowledge

    C. direction   D. instruction

16. The train has left and was soon out of ____.

    A. watch   B. sight

    C. seeing   D. look

17. I have some problems with my English writing. Can you give me some ____?

    A. advice   B. decisions

    C. suggestion   D. messages

18. He thought that his father was old and behind ____.

    A. time   B. the time

    C. a time   D. the times

19. The kind lady was given _____ in return.

    A. two rice   B. two sack rices

    C. two sacks of rice   D. two sack of rice

20. The conference was organized for all of the _____ in the city.

    A. mathematic teachers   B. mathematics's teachers

    C. mathematics' teachers   D. mathematics teachers

21. All my students became _____ after ten years.

    A. grown-up   B. growns-up

    C. growns-ups   D. grown-ups

22. The police is investigating the _____ about the traffic accident.

    A. passer by   B. passers-by

    C. passer-bys   D. passers-bys

23. All the _____ in the hospital will get a rise tomorrow.

    A. women of doctors   B. woman doctors

    C. women doctors   D. doctors of women

24. Last Sunday my family went to _____.

    A. the child's park   B. the children' park

    C. the children's park   D. the childrens' park

25. The woman over there is _____.

    A. Betty and Mary mother   B. Betty and Mary's mother

    C. Betty's and Mary's mother   D. mother of Betty and Mary's

26. We are going to have _____ quiz after we've finished the first five lessons.

    A. a few minutes   B. a few minute

    C. a few minutes'   D. a few minutes's

27. They have got everything ready to make a _____ across the Atlantic.

    A. trip   B. travel

    C. voyage   D. journey

28. Mary never tells anyone what she does for a _____.

    A. job   B. work

    C. life   D. living

29. The car was going at the _____ of 90 kilometers an hour.

    A. pace   B. step

    C. rate   D. race

30. The jet passenger plane can fly at a（n）____ of nearly 30,000 meter above sea level.

A. altitude   B. attitude

C. gratitude   D. latitude

 第二节 代词

一、代词的定义和分类

（1）定义：指代或代替名词或名词短语的词。

（2）分类：指示代词、人称代词、物主代词、反身代词、不定代词、疑问代词和关系代词。

二、代词的用法

（一）指示代词（this, that, these, those）

1. this/these

（1）近指。

This is my pen.

These are my books.

（2）指代下文要提到的事。

Please remember this: No pain, no gain.

2. that/those

（1）远指。

That is her bike.

Those are my sheep.

（2）指代上文刚刚提到的事。

He was ill. That was why he didn't go to school.

3. 打电话时用 this 介绍自己，用 that 询问对方

This is Mike speaking.

Who is that speaking?

4. that/those 常用于比较句型中

The population of China is larger than that of Japan.

The apples in this shop are much cheaper than those in that shop.

（二）人称代词

	单数形式			复数形式		
主格	I	you	he, she, it	we	you	they
宾格	me	you	him, her, it	us	you	them

1. 通常情况下，人称代词作主语用主格，作宾语用宾格，作表语常用宾格

He left his book in the room.

What would you do if you were him?

2. 在强调句式中，若强调的部分为作主语的人称代词，该词用主格形式

It was he who saved the little child.

3. 在形容词或副词原级比较或比较级中，as…as 或 than 后的人称代词用主格、宾格均可

You are taller than her/she（is）.

4. 人称代词 he 和 she 可用以指代动物、国家、船只、大地、月亮或太阳等

The dog waved his tail when he saw his master.

China is a developing country. But she is becoming stronger and stronger.

5. 人称代词的语序

几个人称代词并列作主语时，顺序如下：

单数形式（二、三、一）you, he/she and I。

复数形式（一、二、三）we, you and they。

6. it 的用法

指代前面提到过的事物	The book on the desk is not mine. It is Jim's.
代替前文出现过的指示代词 this/that	——What's that? ——It's a pencil.
指代动物、婴儿或不明身份的人	Look at the baby. Isn't it lovely? Someone is knocking at the door. Please go and see who it is.
指代时间、季节、天气、距离或自然现象等	Spring is coming. It's warmer and warmer. How far it from your school to your home?
用于强调句型中	It was the soldier who/that saved the boy. It was not until his wife came back that he went to bed.
用作形式主语或形式宾语	It was a pity that you didn't come yesterday. I find it easy to work this math problem out.

续表

用于习惯用语中	➤ make it Shall we meet next week? —Yes, let's make it next Sunday. ➤ worth it Don't hesitate about it! It's worth it. ➤ hit it You hit it this time. He's gone to town. ➤ get it I don't get it. Please explain. ➤ as it is We had planed to finish the task today, but as it is we probably won't finish it until next week. ➤ It all depends/that all depends ——Are you going to the countryside for holiday? ——It/That all depends. ➤ It's up to sb. ——Shall we go out for dinner? ——It's up to you.

（三）物主代词

	单数形式			复数形式		
形容词性物主代词	my	your	his, her, its	our	your	their
名词性物主代词	mine	yours	his, hers, its	ours	yours	theirs

（1）形容词性物主代词后加名词，一般不单独使用；名词性物主代词后不需要加名词，相当于"形容词性物主代词＋名词"。

This is my book.（This book is mine./This book belongs to me.）

（2）名词性物主代词可与 of 连用，构成双重所有格。

He is a friend of mine.

（3）用于"…of one's own"结构中，表示"……自己的"。

She said she had nothing of her own.

（四）反身代词

	单数	复数
第一人称	myself	ourselves
第二人称	yourself	yourselves
第三人称	himself, herself, itself	themselves

1. 反身代词与它所指代的名词或代词在人称、性别、数上保持一致

I hope you can enjoy yourselves at the party.

The children made model planes themselves.

2. 反身代词可作表语、宾语、同位语

That poor boy is myself.

She told the boy to behave himself.

You'd better ask the doctor himself about it.

3. 常用短语

enjoy oneself 玩得开心，过得愉快

say to oneself 自言自语，心中暗想

teach oneself/learn by oneself 自学

help oneself to… 随便吃 / 喝 / 用……

come to oneself 苏醒

The old woman lives by oneself.（独自）

He has right to decide for himself.（为自己）

This is not a bad idea in itself.（本身）

She will not give up of herself.（自动地）

（五）疑问代词

用来引导特殊疑问句	who, whom, whose, what, which
用来引导名词性从句	whoever, whomever, whichever, whatever

1. 疑问代词引导特殊疑问句

（1）who, whom, whose：用于指人，可作主语、宾语、表语或定语。

Who can answer the question?

Who/Whom did you borrow the bike from?

Whose is this shirt?

Whose shirt is this?

（2）what：用于指物，可作主语、宾语、表语或定语。

What has happened?

What do you mean?

What time shall we meet again?

（3）which：既用于指人，也用于指物，可作主语、宾语或定语。

Which do you prefer?

Which of you will go there with me?

Which job are you applying for?

（4）whoever, whomever, whichever, whatever：分别为 who, whom, which, what 的强调形式，意为"到底，究竟"。

Whoever told you that?

Whomever did you give the money to?

Whichever book is yours?

Whatever did you hear?

2. 疑问代词引导名词性从句

Whatever I have is yours.

What I want to know is which one he wants.

Do you know who broke the window?

（六）不定代词

普通不定代词	both, either, neither, each, all, none, some, any, other, the other, others, the others, another, many, much
复合不定代词	someone/somebody, anyone/anybody, no one/nobody, everyone/everybody
	something, anything, nothing, everything

> 普通不定代词

1. some, any

（1）意为"一些、若干"，既可修饰可数名词，也可修饰不可数名词。some 一般用于肯定句，any 多用于否定句和疑问句。

Some children were playing in the park.

Some of his stories were quite amusing.

Is there any water left in the glass?

（2）在疑问句中，当表示说话人希望得到肯定回答或表达请求、建议时用 some。

Would you like some coffee?

（3）any 和单数可数名词或不可数名词连用，意为"任何一个"，用于肯定句。

They will need any help they can get.

（4）some 与单数可数名词连用，意为"某个"。

There must be some reason for what she's done.

2. many, much

（1）many 作代词代表可数名词，much 作代词代表不可数名词。

Many of his ideas were amusing to her.

Much of the land was flooded.

（2）many 作形容词修饰可数名词，much 修饰不可数名词。

I recall many discussions with her on these topics.

He doesn't spend much time preparing his lessons.

（3）too many "太多"，后加复数可数名词。

There are too many errors in your work.

too much "太多"，后加不可数名词。

I think the problem can be got over without too much difficulty.

much too "太……"，后加形容词或副词。

The clothes she wears are much too young for her.

3. each, every

（1）each 强调个体，作主语时谓语动词用单数；every 强调整体情况，修饰名词作主语时谓语动词也用单数形式。

Each of us wears a yellow T-shirt.

Every student in Class 5 has passed the exam.

（2）each 指两个或两个以上的人或事物，every 指三个或三个以上的人或事物。

There are trees on each side of the road.

（3）every 可以用于 "every+ 基数词 + 复数名词" 或 "every+ 序数词 + 单数名词" 结构中，表示 "每隔……" "每……"，each 不能用于此结构中。

every five days=every fifth day   every three years=every third year

（4）every+other+ 单数名词，意为 "每隔一……" 或 "每两……"。

He went to see his parents every other year.

You should write on every other line.Each has his advantages.

4. both, either, neither, all, none

（1）both 两者都。

① both of + 人称代词宾格 / 修饰限定词 + 复数名词（作主语时，谓语动词用复数形式）。

Both of us are students.

=We are both students.

Both of the students like English.

The students both like English.

② both A and B　　A 和 B 都……（作主语时，谓语动词用复数形式）。

I like both English and math.

Both Peter and Mary are students.

※not only… but also… 不仅……而且……

Not only Bob but I am doing housework.

=Both Bob and I are doing housework.

（2）either（两者）任何一个。

① either of + 人称代词宾格 / 修饰限定词 + 复数名词（作主语时谓语动词用单数）。

Either of us is a student.

=Both of us are students.

② either A or B　　要么 A 要么 B（作主语时谓语动词遵循就近原则）。

Either you or I am right.

（3）neither（两者）都不……

① neither of + 人称代词宾格 / 复数名词（作主语时谓语动词用单数或复数）。

Neither of us is/are wrong.

Neither of the boys likes/like P. E.

② neither A nor B 既不……也不……，A 和 B 都不……（作主语时谓语动词遵循就近原则）。

My father neither smokes nor drinks.

Neither Peter nor I am wrong.

（4）all（三者或三者以上）全都、所有的。

① all（of）一般放在名词和代词前面。当名词前面有限定词（如 the, my, this…），all/all of 都可用，作主语时谓语动词的单复数形式取决于名词。

All（of）the money has been spent.

All（of）the students have gone to Beijing.

② 当名词前面没有限定词时，一般使用 all。

All children can be naughty sometimes.

③ 当名词前面有人称代词时，一般使用 all of。

All of them can come tomorrow.

④ 固定搭配。

→ all your life/all day/all year 一生 / 一整天 / 整年

He had worked all his life in the mine.

The boys played video games all day.

→ at all 完全（不），一点（都不）

They've done nothing at all to try and put the problem right.

→ all but 几乎，差不多

Britain's coal industry has all but disappeared.

His left arm was all but useless.

（5）none（三者或三者以上）都不……

① 单独使用，后面不加名词，代替上文中出现的名词，相当于 no+ 名词。

——Have you any money?

——No, I have none（no money）.

I haven't got any beer. / I've got no beer. / I've got none.

② none of+ 人称代词宾格 / 复数名词（作主语时谓语动词可用单数或复数）。

None of us is/are students.

5. the other, the others, other, others, another

（1）other 另外的。

作定语，常与复数名词连用；若前面有 the, some, any, each, every, no, my, your, his 等，则可与单数名词连用。

I don't care what other people may think of me.

（2）the other（两者中的）另一个。

常与 one 连用，构成 "one..., the other..."；作定语修饰复数名词时，表示 "其余的全部"。

He has two daughters. One is a teacher, the other is a doctor.

（3）others 另一些。

泛指别的人或物（但不是全部），不能作定语，可构成 some...others... 结构。

Some of them are for the plan while others are against it.

（4）the others 其余的。

特指其余所有的人或物。

Some students come from China, the others from America.

（5）another 另一个。

① 指三者或三者以上之中的任何一个，用作限定词或代词。

Would you like another cup of coffee?

② another + 数词 + 复数名词意为 "再……"，相当于 "数词 +more+ 复数名词" 或 "数词 + 复数名词 + more"。

In another three weeks he will come back.

We walked another ten miles.

> 复合不定代词

表示"人"的复合不定代词		表示"物"的复合不定代词
someone	somebody	something
anyone	anybody	anything
everyone	everybody	everything
no one	nobody	nothing

（1）someone/somebody, something 常用于肯定句和委婉表达的疑问句中。（Could you…/May I…/Would you like…/Can you（I）…; anyone/anybody, anything 常用于疑问句和否定句。

Would you like something to eat?

Is there anything wrong with your bike?

There ins't anything wrong with my bike.

（2）复合不定代词作主语时，谓语动词用单数形式。

Everyone likes playing games.

（3）形容词 /else/to do 与复合不定代词连用时，放在其后面。

There is something interesting in today's newspaper.

There is something wrong with my eyes.

I have something else to tell you.

Would you like something to eat/drink?

（4）not anyone=no one, not anybody=nobody, not anything=nothing。

There ins't anything in the box. = There is nothing in the box.

I can't see anybody. = I can see nobody.

（5）主语是复合不定代词的反义疑问句。

① 如果陈述句的主语是指代"物"的复合不定代词，反义疑问句的主语用 it。

② 如果陈述句的主语是指代"人"的符合不定代词，反义疑问句的主语用 he（强调个体）或 they（强调整体）。

Everything is ready, ins't it?

Someone is singing, ins't he?

Everybody is in the classroom, aren't they?

（6）常见含复合不定代词的习惯搭配。

The building is something like a church.　　　　（有点像）

There were something like 100 people present.　　（大约）

He is something of a musician. （有点儿，有几分）

He is a teacher or something. （类似的，表示不确定）

She is anything but a scholar. （根本不，绝非）

She is nothing but a scholar. （只是）

（七）关系代词

关系代词包括：who, whom, whose, which, that, as 等，用来引导定语从句。

A postman is a man who/that delivers letters.

She said she'd been waiting for an hour, which was true.

This is the book which/that I told you about.

That's the man whose house was burnt down.

专项练习题

一、用所给单词的适当形式填空

1. These are my colour pencils. Where are ____（you）?

2. Kate, help ____（you）to some fish, please.

3. They planted many trees; all of ____（they）were taken good care of.

4. Our work is not so good as ____（he）.

5.They told us about their school and we told them about ____（we）.

6. Joe, Bill and ____（I）went to school together.

7. Kate and her sister went to holiday with a friend of ____（they）.

8. I mistook ____（she）to be mine.

9. Don't shake the young trees. ____（it）leaves are falling off.

10. William has two daughters and he loves both of ____（they）.

二、单项选择题

1. An old friend of my father's always helps my brother and ____ with ____ maths.

    A. I, our   B. me, ourselves

    C. I, my   D. me, our

2. Let ____ promise not to quarrel about such an unimportant matter any more.

    A. you and I   B. I and you

    C. me and you   D. you and me

3. We must protect plants because they are friends of ____.

    A. we   B. us

    C. our   D. ours

4. ——Who taught your brother to surf?

    ——Nobody. He learnt all by ____.

    A. him   B. himself

    C. me   D. myself

5. Jack is going to have ____ examined, for he is not quite ____ today.

    A. him, him   B. him, himself

    C. himself, him   D. himself, himself

6. Come in, Jane. Make ____ at home.

    A. you   B. yourself

    C. yourselves   D. your

7. ——Mary plays the piano very well.

    ——Does she? I didn't know____.

    A. that   B. this

    C. it   D. these

8. ——This is Linda speaking. ____?

    ——This is Bill.

    A. Who are you   B. Who is he

    C. Are you Bill   D. Who's that

9. There are so many kinds of computers on sale that I can't decide ____ to buy.

    A. what   B. which

    C. how   D. where

10. ——____ is in charge of the summer concert?

    ——Jessie. She has a lot of experience.

    A. Where   B. Why

    C. What   D. Who

11. I'm sorry I know ____ about it. It's a secret between them.

    A. nothing   B. something

    C. anything   D. everything

12. I've been so bored for a long time. I hope to have ____ to do.

    A. exciting anything   B. nothing exciting

C. something interesting   D. good something

13. I tried two bookstores for the book I wanted, but _____ of them had it.

    A. none   B. either

    C. neither   D. both

14. There ins't _____ paper in the printer. Will you get _____ for me?

    A. any, some   B. any, any

    C. some, some   D. some, any

15. This is not my umbrella. I must have taken _____ umbrella by mistake.

    A. somebody else   B. somebody else's

    C. somebody's else's   D. somebody's else

16. ——When are we going to see a movie, this afternoon or tonight?

    ——_____ is OK. I'm free today.

    A. Either   B. Neither

    C. Both   D. All

17. At the beginning of the term, I found _____ difficult to study English.

    A. that   B. its

    C. it   D. this

18. ——Who is singing in the next room?

    ——_____ must be Julie.

    A. She   B. It

    C. That   D. There

19. Look at the dark clouds. _____ going to rain.

    A. It's   B. It

    C. Its   D. It was

20. I think it is no use _____ the reason to him.

    A. explaining   B. to explain

    C. explain   D. explained

21. Both Tony and Scott have told me about it, but I don't believe _____.

    A. some   B. either

    C. neither   D. each

22. The soldiers became tired of fighting and began to quarrel among _____.

    A. them   B. themselves

    C. each other   D. one another

23. A good teacher is ____ who has both rich knowledge and virtues.

    A. one   B. this

    C. that   D. he

24. My boyfriend and I meet ____ week.

    A. any other   B. every other

    C. other   D. the other

25. The air in a country is usually much cleaner than____ in the city.

    A. the one   B. that

    C. those   D. this

26. I can't go. For one thing I have seen the film; for ____ I have an important appointment.

    A. other   B. the other

    C. others   D. another

27. Some went to the Summer Palace, ____ visited the Great Wall.

    A. other   B. others

    C. another   D. the other

28. My parents ____ in tonight.

    A. are both   B. all are

    C. both are   D. are all

29. After a long walk I wanted to drink____.

    A. cold something   B. some cold things

    C. something cold   D. something to make cold

30. ____ is what I mean: You should have come earlier.

    A. That   B. This

    C. It   D. Those

第三节 冠词

一、冠词的定义和分类

（1）定义：置于名词之前，说明名词所表示的人或事物的词。

（2）分类：不定冠词、定冠词、零冠词。

二、不定冠词

不定冠词有 a 和 an 两种形式，只用于单数可数名词前。a 用于以辅音音素开头的词前面，an 用于以元音音素开头的词前面，不定冠词主要表示类指和数量的意义。

（一）基本用法

1. 用于单数可数名词前，表示"一类人或物"

A child needs love.

A square has four sides.

2. 用于作表语的单数可数名词前，说明某人的身份、职业或某物的类别

He is an American.（=He is American.）

Her wish is to become a teacher.

It is a pen, not a ballpoint pen.

3. 用于第一次提到的人或物的单数可数名词前

There is a man waiting for you outside. The man looks worried.

I looked up and saw a bird. The bird flew low over the trees.

4. 表示"一"这个数量，与数词 one 意义相同，但不像 one 那样强调数字

He needs an assistant.

5. 用于表示价格、速度、时间等名词前，表示"每一"，相当于 each 或 per

My mother goes shopping once a week.

The car travels at one hundred miles an hour.

6. 用于一些名词前，表示"同一，相同"的意思

My coat and his are of a size.

The two girls are of an age.

7. 用于表姓氏的专有名词前，表明说话者不认识此人，意为"一个叫……的人"；不定冠词用于表示日期、地点的专有名词前，含有"特定"的意思

There is a Mrs. Smith on the phone for you.

I can't remember a Christmas when it snowed so much.

8. 用于一些通常成对出现的名词前，这些名词往往被看作一个整体

Have you got a needle and thread here?

I need a knife and fork to use for my breakfast.

9. 用于一些表示疾病的名词前，与 have 构成短语，表示"得……病"

have a cold	have a headache	have a toothache
have/run a fever	have a stomachache	have a backache
have a temperature	have an earache	have a sore throat

※ have flu（得流感）

10. 用于序数词前，表示"又一，再一"的意思

Shall I ask a third time?

When I sat down, a fourth man rose to speak.

（二）固定短语

as a matter of fact	at a loss	in a sense
all of a sudden	at a discount	in a hurry
as a rule	for a while	in a word
have a word with	keep an eye on	make a living
lend a hand	have a good time	as a result
keep a diary	do sb. a favor	pay a visit
have a look /talk/swim/rest/break/try/drink		

三、定冠词

定冠词可以用于单（复）数可数名词和不可数名词前，表示类指、特指等意义。

（一）基本用法

1. 用于单数可数名词前，表示"一类人或物"

The whale is in danger of becoming extinct.

The telephone was invented by Alexander G. Bell.

※ 不定冠词和定冠词都可以表示类属。不定冠词强调个体，相当于 every；定冠词强调类别，相当于 all。若一类事物中的个体可以代表整体的特征，则二者可以互换使用。

The whale is in danger of becoming extinct.

A horse is a useful animal.（=Every horse is a useful animal.）

=The horse is a useful animal.（=All horses are useful animals.）

2. 用于某些形容词或分词前，表示"一类人或情况"

The rich get richer and the poor get poorer.

She attended to the wounded day and night.

We love the true, the good and the beautiful.

3. 用于上文提到的人或物的名词前

He ordered some books last month. The books have arrived now.

We have a cat and two dogs; the cat is black and the dogs are white.

4. 表示谈话双方都知道的特定人或物

Where's Helen? —She is in the garden.

Would you pass me the vinegar, please?

5. 用于表姓氏的复数名词前，表示"一家人"

The Smiths often go swimming on Sundays.

The Greens were too poor to send their son to school.

6. 用于形容词（副词）最高级，序数词或 next, last, only, main, sole, same 等前面

He is the cleverest boy in his class.

The boy runs（the）fastest among the three.

He is the first man to come here.

This is the only way to solve the problem.

They both said the same thing.

7. 用于由短语或从句修饰的名词前

The key to the safe is lost.

This is the room where the meeting was held.

8. 表示整体中的部分，如人体部分的 the mind, the brain, the heart 等；物体部分的 the door, the street, the inside 等

The view there is sweet to the eye and the mind.

Be careful when you cross the street.

That car tried to pass me on the inside.

9. 用于表示世界上独一无二的事物前，如 sun, moon, universe, world, sky, earth, sea 等

The sea covers more than half the surface of the earth.

When did the universe come into being?

10. 用于方位名词前

Birds come back from the south in spring.

It's very cold in winter in the north.

11. 用于表示"动词 + 宾语 + 介词（in, on, by）+the+ 身体部位"，表示"击打……"

She hit him in the face.（=She hit his face.）

He patted the boy on the head.（=He patted the boy's head.）

※ He grasped her by the collar.（=He grasped her collar.）

12. 表示世纪中的年代

The war broke out in the 1980s.

In the fifties（50s），there weren't so many people.

13. 用于西洋乐器名称的名词前

She is learning to play the violin.

He plays the guitar very well.

14. 用于海洋、河流、山脉、群岛、某些国名、组织机构、报纸、书籍、条约等名词前

the Atlantic	the Thames	the New York Times
the U.S.A	the CPC	the WTO
the Daily Telegraph	the Bible	the Treaty of Nanjing

（二）固定短语

at the same time	on the spot	to tell the truth
on t he other hand	on the whole	for the time being
all the year round	break the ice	in the long run
in the daytime	in the end	all the time
by the way	at the age of	in the open air
at the beginning of	on the other side of	at the moment
in the middle of	in the morning/afternoon/evening	

四、零冠词

某些名词前面不使用冠词，这种情况又称为零冠词。零冠词只用于不可数名词、复数可数名词前，主要表示类指、特指等意义。

（一）基本用法

1. 不可数名词和复数名词表示泛指时

Animal can't live without water.

Electricity is a form of energy.

Life is short; art is long.

Woman is frail.

2. 某些专有名词，如人名、地名、国家名表示泛指时

China is a great country.

Mary lives in New York.

3. 名词前已有指示代词、物主代词或名词所有格等修饰

Every student likes English in our class.

4. 用于称呼语或表示头衔的名词前

This is Professor Li.

5. 用在日期、月份、季节、节假日、日（夜）时段、一日三餐的名词前

March is my favorite month.

If winter comes, can spring be far behind?

Christmas is the time for family reunion.

I went to school without breakfast this morning.

6. 用在球类运动、游戏、语言、学科名词之前

He often plays football after school.

Shall we play chess?

He majors in history.

7. 用在"专有名词 + 普通名词"构成的表示街名、路名、山名等的词前面

Hainan Island   Nanjing Road

8. by 与交通工具或通讯方式连用时

by car/ train/ taxi   by water/sea/boat/ship

by air/（aero）plane   by post/letter/telegram

9. 在由 as/though 引导的让步状语从句中，用于置于句首的名词前

Young boy as he was, he knew a lot about the world.

Fool as he looks, he always seems to make the wisest suggestions.

10. 某些独立结构中，名词前往往要使用零冠词

Mrs. Smith sat at the desk, coat off, head down, and pen in（her）hand.

The old man was standing by the road, pipe in（his）mouth.

（二）固定搭配

day and night	face to face	side by side
step by step	at school/work/home	at first/last
in trouble	in danger	on foot
on duty/watch	in bed	in time
on time	at night/noon/ dawn	in prison
lose heart	by chance	catch sight of
on account of	make use of	keep in mind
on hand	in spite of	from top to bottom

➤ 知识点拓展

有定冠词和无定冠词的区别：

1. go to school 去上学（身份是学生）   2. go to bed 上床睡觉

go to the school 去学校（身份不确定）   go to the bed 向床边走去（不一定去睡觉）

3. at table 在吃饭

   at the table 在桌子旁边

4. at school 在上学

   at the school 在学校里

5. in class 在上课

   in the class 在班级里

6. in future 今后

   in the future 将来

7. in front of 在……（外部的）前面

   in the front of 在……（内部的）前面

8. next year 明年

   the next year 第二年

9. by sea 乘船

   by the sea 在海边

10. take place 发生

   take the place（of）代替

11. go to church 去做礼拜

   go to the church 到教堂去

12. on horseback 骑着马

   on the horseback 在马背上

13. two fo us 我们当中的两人

   the two of us 我们两人（共计两人）

14. out of question 毫无疑问

   out of the question 不可能，不值得讨论

专项练习题

一、用 a, an, the 或 / 填空

1. There will be ____ strong wind in South China.

2. I'm going to make ____ special house for my pet pig this weekend.

3. ____ Room 205 is on ____ second floor.

4. My uncle is ____ engineer. He works very hard.

5. ____ Smiths are watching TV now.

6. Atacama Desert is one of ____ driest places in ____ Africa.

7. My mother was born in ____1980s.

8. We elected Tony ____ monitor of our class.

9. My favorite subject at school was ____ chemistry.

10. The room is four times ____ size of that one.

11. We visited ____ Summer Palace last month.

12. It takes us about ____ hour to get to the airport from my flat by ____ taxi.

13. What do you think of ____ music in the film we saw yesterday?

14. I like ____ music, especially ____ classical music.

15. There is ____"U" in ____ word "use".

二、单项选择题

1. ——Who's _____ boy in blue, do you know?

   ——Oh, he's _____ friend of Tom.

   A. the, a   B. an, the

   C. a, the   D. the, an

2. We will see _____ even stronger China in _____ near future.

   A. a, the   B. an, the

   C. the, a   D. an, a

3. How wonderfully she sings! I have never heard _____.

   A. the best voice   B. a good voice

   C. the better voice   D. a better voice

4. _____ Father's Day is coming. Jerry will buy a new wallet for his father.

   A. A   B. An

   C. The   D. /

5. ——What's _____ trouble with you?

   ——have _____ trouble with my throat.

   A. /, the   B. the, /

   C. the, the   D. /, /

6. France is _____ only European country I have ever visited.

   A. a   B. an

   C. the   D. /

7. Benjamin Franklin discovered _____ electricity and John Baird invented television.

   A. an, a   B. /, the

   C. the, /   D. /, /

8. As we know, England is _____ European country and Singapore is _____ Asian country.

   A. an, an   B. an, a

   C. a, a   D. a, an

9. It has been _____ to talk with you.

   A. pleasure   B. pleasures

   C. the pleasure   D. a pleasure

10. Beijing, _____ capital of China, has _____ long history.

    A. a, a   B. the, /

C. the, a   D. /, the

11. ——Did you have ____ breakfast?

　　——Yes, I have ____ nice breakfast.

　　A.a, a   B. /, /

　　C. a, /   D. /, a

12. He usually went to school by ____ bike, but today he went to school in ____taxi.

　　A. /, /   B. /, a

　　C. a, /   D. a, a

13. ——How about ____ talent show?

　　——I should say it was ____ great success.

　　A./, the   B. a, the

　　C. the, a   D. the, /

14. ——Shall we pay ____ visit to the Science Museum?

　　——No, I'd rather stay at home and play ____ football.

　　A.a, the   B. the, a

　　C. /, the   D. a, /

15. ____ teacher and ____ scholar has accepted the invitation.

　　A. The, the   B. /, the

　　C. The, /   D. /, /

16. My brother Bred woke up with ____ bad headache, yet by the evening the pain had gone.

　　A. a   B. an

　　C. the   D. /

17. If you go by train, you can have quite ____ comfortable journey, but make sure you take ____ fast one.

　　A. a, a   B. the, a

　　C. the, the   D. /, a

18. There's ____800-metre-long road behind ____ hospital.

　　A. an, an   B. a, a

　　C. an, the   D. a, the

19. When he was playing, a ball hit him ____.

　　A. on a nose   B. on the nose

　　C. in the nose   D. in a nose

20. Let's take ____ to do the work.

    A. a turn   B. the turn

    C. our turn   D. turns

21. Every one of us has ____ machine; ____ machine is ____ brain.

    A. a, the, the   B. a, a, a

    C. a, a, the   D. the, a, a

22. They come to see us at least ____.

    A. once the year   B. once a year

    C. one time in a year   D.one time the year

23. ____ Mr. Jones called while you were out. He was in ____ very bad temper.

    A. The, a   B. A, /

    C. The, the   D. A, a

24. ____ was all he asked for.

    A. The bread and the butter   B. Bread and butter

    C. The bread and butter   D. A bread and butter

25. Gun in ____ hand, the soldiers searched for the escaped enemy.

    A. a   B.one

    C. the   D. /

26. In order to promote the new products, they persuaded people to buy them ____ .

    A. from the door to the door   B. from a door to a door

    C. from a door to another   D. from door to door

27. ____ honest boy as he was, he didn't study hard.

    A. /   B. A

    C. The   D. An

28. ____ to be taken good care of.

    A. Young are   B. Young is

    C. Young people is   D. The young are

29. Later, the chance to enter ____ came and he took it.

    A. into college   B. to college

    C. into the college   D. college

30. Signals are made ____ with flags and ____ with lights.

    A. by the day，by the night   B. by day，by night

    C. by night,by day   D. by the night,by the day

第四节 数词

一、数词的定义和分类

（1）定义：表示数目多少或顺序先后的词。

（2）分类：基数词：表示数量 one, two, three…

序数词：表示顺序 first, second, third…

二、数词的语法功能

数词可在句子中作主语、表语、宾语、定语、同位语和状语等。

The first is better than the second.

She was the third to arrive.

We three failed the English exam.

When did you first meet him?

三、基数词变序数词

数字	基数词	序数词	序数词的缩写
1	one	first	1st
2	two	second	2nd
3	three	third	3rd
4	four	fourth	4th
5	five	fifth	5th
6	six	sixth	6th
7	seven	seventh	7th
8	eight	eighth	8th
9	nine	ninth	9th
10	ten	tenth	10th
11	eleven	eleventh	11th
12	twelve	twelfth	12th
13	thirteen	thirteenth	13th
14	fourteen	fourteenth	14th
15	fifteen	fifteenth	15th
20	twenty	twentieth	20th
21	twenty-one	twenty-first	21st

续表

数字	基数词	序数词	序数词的缩写
22	twenty-two	twenty-second	22nd
23	twenty-three	twenty-third	23rd
24	twenty-four	twenty-fourth	24th
25	twenty-five	twenty-fifth	25th
26	twenty-six	twenty-sixth	26th
27	twenty-seven	twenty-seventh	27th
28	twenty-eight	twenty-eighth	28th
29	twenty-nine	twenty-ninth	29th
30	thirty	thirtieth	30th

※ 基数词变序数词规则巧记

1、2、3，特殊记；8 去 t，9 去 e；ve 要用 f 替；如果以 y 来结尾，先变 y 为 i 和 e；th 最后加上去。

四、基数词与序数词的用法

（一）基数词的构成

（1）1~12 为独立单词，分别用 one, two, three, four, five, six, seven, eight, nine, ten, eleven, twelve 表示；13~19 以后缀 -teen 结尾，分别用 thirteen, fourteen, fifteen, sixteen, seventeen, eighteen, nineteen 表示；20~90 以后缀 -ty 结尾，分别用 twenty, thirty, forty, fifty, sixty, seventy, eighty, ninety 表示。

（2）百—hundred、千—thousand、百万—million、十亿—billion、兆—trillion。

（3）十位与个位之间需用连字符隔开。

43 → forty-three   21 → twenty-one

（4）百位与十位之间用 and 连接。

637 → six hundred and thirty-seven

（二）四位以上数字的读法

1,	234,	567,	890
billion,	million,	thousand,	hundred

读成：one billion, two hundred and thirty-four million, five hundred and sixty-seven thousand, eight hundred and ninety

（三）用法

1. hundred, thousand, million 等词的用法

（1）与具体数词或 several, some, many 连用时用单数形式。

two hundred teachers	two dozen（of）eggs
five score（of）students	three score and ten years

（2）表示"好几十、成百上千、成千上万"等不确的数字时，与 of 连用，用复数形式。

dozens/scores of times	hundreds of people
tens of thousands of ants	millions of birds

2. 基数词表示钟表上的时间

（1）直接表达法。

6:00	six（o'clock）
9:25	nine twenty–five a.m.
12:30	twelve thirty p.m.

（2）间接表达法。

用 past/after（过），to/of（差）也可以表示时刻，"过"或"差"的时间一般限定在 30 分钟以内。

9:25	twenty–five past/after nine a.m.
12:30	thirty past/after twelve（=half past/after twelve）
7:45	fifteen to/of eight（=a quarter to/of eight）

3. 基数词表示年代

（1）2022 年	two thousand and twenty– two
1989 年	nineteen eighty–nine（=nineteen hundred and eighty–nine）
1980's（1980s）	nineteen eighties
73A.D.（A.D.73）	seventy–three A.D.
345B.C.（B.C.345）	three forty–five B.C.（=three hundred and forty–five B.C.）

（2）用于"in the + 基数词复数形式"结构中：

in the early twenties

in the eighties of last century

4. 基数词表示书页、住所、房间、教室，电话号码等

Lesson 5（=the fifth lesson）

Page three（=P.3=the third page）

Unit two（=the second unit）

Part one（=the first part）

Room 301

Number 5（No.5）

2839096（电话号码）two eight three, nine O nine, six

5. 基数词表示数学公式

2+3=5　　Two plus three is/are/equals/is equal to/makes/make five.

　　　　　Two and three is/are/equals/is equal to/makes/make five.

10﹣4=6　Ten minus four is six.

　　　　　Four from ten leaves/is six.

7×3=21　Seven times/multiplied by three is twenty–one.

　　　　　Seven threes are twenty–one.

9÷3=3　　Nine divided by three is three.

6. 基数词表示人的大概年龄，用于"in +one's+ 基数词复数"结构中

He died in his sixties.

She is still in her early/middle/late twenties.

He is in his early/late teens.

7. 表示"每，每隔"的意义，用于"every+ 基数词 + 复数名词"和"every+ 序数词 + 单数名词"结构中

every four days / every fourth day（每 4 天或每隔 3 天）

every ten meters / every tenth day（每 10 米或每隔 9 米）

every other day, every two days / every second day（每隔 1 天）

every few days 　　（隔些日子）

8. 表示日期

汉语中日期的表达顺序是：年﹣月﹣日

例如，2021 年 3 月 27 日。

英语中日期的表达顺序有以下两种：

（1）月﹣日﹣年：

March 27 th/ 27, 2021

读法：March（the）twenty–seventh, twenty twenty–one

（2）日﹣月﹣年：

27th/27 March, 2021

读法：the twenty–seven of March, 2021

12 个月份的表达		
January（一月）	February（二月）	March（三月）
April（四月）	May（五月）	June（六月）

12 个月份的表达		
July（七月）	August（八月）	September（九月）
October（十月）	November（十一月）	December（十二月）

9. 序数词前面通常加定冠词 the

I like the first car.

I'm the first.

※ 如果序数词前面有形容词性物主代词（my, your, his, her...），名词所有格（Peter's）等词修饰时，则定冠词 the 省略。

This is my first car.

My sister is five years old. Today is her fifth birthday.

There are eight floors in this building. And I live on the third floor.

10. 序数词和不定冠词连用时，此时不定冠词表示"再一，又一"的意思。

We have to do it a second time.

When I sat down, a third person rose to speak.

五、分数、小数、百分数和倍数

（一）分数

分子用基数词，分母用序数词。当分子大于 1 时，分母的序数词用复数形式。整数和分数之间用 and 连接。当分子和分母都较大时，分子和分母用基数词表示，中间用 over 连接。

$\dfrac{7}{8}$ → seven eighths　　　　　　$\dfrac{1}{2}$ → one half

$\dfrac{1}{4}$ → one–fourth（one quarter）　　$\dfrac{3}{4}$ → three–fourths（three quarters）

$3\dfrac{5}{6}$ → three and five–sixths　　　$\dfrac{25}{87}$ → twenty–five over eighty–seven

（二）小数

小数用基数词表示，以小数点为界，小数点读作 point。小数点前面的数字为一个单位，表示整数，数字合起来读。小数点后面的数字为另一个单位，表示小数，数字分开读。

0 读作 zero 或 o; 整数部分为零时，可省略不读。

2.16　　　　　two point one six

0.4　　　　　zero point four（或 point four）

15.87　　　　fifteen point eight seven

1.03   one point o three

（三）百分数

用"基数词 +percent"表示。

0.5%   zero point five percent

45%   forty–five percent

82.07%   eighty–two point zero seven percent

※ percentage 与 percent 的区别

percentage 意为"百分比、百分率"，一般不与具体数字连用。如表示百分之几，需用"基数词 +percent"。

According to a recent survey, the percentage of working women is stuck at 32%.

（四）倍数

1. N+times + 名词 +of

The apples are three times the weight of the pears.

The earth is 49 times the size of the moon.

2. N+times +as+ 形容词（副词）+as

The room is twice as wide as that one.

Our college is three times as large as theirs.

3. N+times + 形容词（副词）比较级 + than

The oil output this year is four times greater than that of last year.

This apple is three times bigger than that one.

4. "increase+（to/by）+N+times/fold" "increase+ by+ a factor of N" 表示"增加到 N 倍，增加了 N–1 倍"

This will increased the speed ten times（=tenfold）as against 2005.

The voltage has been increased by a factor of four.

The output of grain went up by three times over the previous year.

5. "decrease+（by）+N+times/fold" "decrease+ by+ a factor of N" 结构均表示"减少到 1/ N，减少了（N–1）/ N"

Industrial accidents decreased three times（=threefold）this year.

The equipment reduced the error probability by a factor of 5.

专项练习题

一、用所给单词的适当形式填空

1. Today we are going to learn the ＿＿＿（ twelve ）lesson.

2. I wonder if I can have a ＿＿＿（ three ）cake.

3. The Great Wall was built ＿＿＿（ thousand ）of years ago.

4. Eric's parents are holding a party to celebrate his ＿＿＿（ nine ）birthday.

5. There are ＿＿＿（ seven ）days in a week.

6. He is the ＿＿＿（ four ）tallest in our class.

7. He has two ＿＿＿（ hundred ）dollars.

8. Chester Alan Arthur was the ＿＿＿（ twenty-one ）president of the United States.

9. Pass me the book. The ＿＿＿（ two ）one.

10. I was the ＿＿＿（ one ）one to come to school today.

二、单项选择题

1. ＿＿＿ month of the year if May.

   A. Two   B. The second

   C. Five   D. The fifth

2. For breakfast, I usually have ＿＿＿ and two pieces of bread.

   A. a cup of milk half   B. half a cup of milk

   C. a half milk cup   D. half a milk cup

3. Nowadays about ＿＿＿ of business letters are written in English.

   A. two third   B. two thirds

   C. two three   D. second three

4. You can see ＿＿＿ if you go out at night.

   A. million stars   B. thousand of stars

   C. hundreds stars   D. millions of stars

5. More than nine ＿＿＿ students are doing sports in the playground now.

   A. hundreds   B. hundred of

   C. hundred   D. hundreds of

6. I don't believe that this ＿＿＿ boy can paint such a nice picture.

   A. five years old   B. five-year-old

   C. five-years-old   D. five year old

7. The hero of the story is a soldier in his ____.

    A. thirtieth   B. thirty

    C. thirty's   D. thirties

8. China, ____ largest country in the world, has a population of ____.

    A. third, 140 million   B. the third, one point four billion

    C. the third, 140 million   D. third, one point four billion

9. John was in London on the ____ of May.

    A. twenty-two   B. twentieth-two

    C. twenty-second   D. twentieth-second

10. The story happened in ____.

    A. the 1990s   B. 1990s

    C. 1990's   D. the 1990

11. After the new technique was introduced, the factory produced ____ cars in 2019 as the year before.

    A. as many twice   B. as twice many

    C. twice as many   D. twice many as

12. Our teacher advised us to try it ____ time.

    A. the third   B. a third

    C. three   D. the three

13. The Russian teacher has been in our school for ____.

    A. one and the half year   B. one year and a half

    C. one and half year   D. one year and a half year

14. My mother paid twenty yuan for ____ eggs.

    A. two dozen and five   B. two dozens and five

    C. two dozen and six of   D. two dozen of and five

15. ——David, how old is your father this year?

    ——____. And we just had a special party for his ____ birthday last weekend.

    A. Fortieth, forty   B. Forty, forty

    C. Forty, fortieth   D. Fortieth, fortieth

16. ——Good morning, madam. Can I help you?

    ——Sure, I'd like ____ for cooking vegetables.

    A. two cups of tea   B. three pieces of bread

    C. five kilos of oil   D. four bottles of juice

17. Nearly ____ of the earth ____ covered by sea.

    A. three fourth, is   B. three fourths, is

    C. three fourth, are   D. three fourths, are

18. Are these seats for us ____?

    A. the third   B. three

    C. third   D. the three

19. The old man began to learn to drive a car at the age of ____.

    A. sixty   B. the sixtieth

    C. sixty years old   D. sixties

20. ——Excuse me, sir. Here's a package for Lin Tao. Which room does he live in?

    ——____ ____.

    A. 308 Room   B. Room 308

    C. The Room 308   D. The 308 Room

21. The work is too difficult for Mr. Zhu to finish in a week. He needs ____ days.

    A. more two   B. two more

    C. two another   D. another more

22. ——Shanghai has opened its ____ TV channel that sends programs in foreign languages.

    ——Great! I can improve my English over it.

    A. first   B. a first

    C. the first   D. first's

23. The weight of the moon is only about ____ of the earth.

    A. one eight   B. one of eight

    C. one the eighties   D. one eightieth

24. My friend was born ____.

    A. in 2006, June   B. in June, 2006

    C. on June, 2006   D. June, 2006

25. ____ the students usually surf on the Internet and get information.

    A. 60 percent of   B. 60 percent

    C. 60 percents of   D. 60 percents

26. The First World War broke out in ____.

    A. 1914   B. 1914s

    C. 1914's   D. the 1914

27. ——What time do you usually get up, John?

      ——I usually get up at ____.

      A. half past six   B. half to six

      C. half after six   D. half before six

28. The rope is ____ that one.

      A. four times longer   B. three times the length of

      C. twice so long as   D. three times than

29. Shakespeare was born in ____.

      A. 1660s   B. the 1660

      C. the 1660's   D. 1660's

30. ——How far is your cousin's home from here?

      ——It's about ____ drive.

      A. two hours   B two hour's

      C. two hours'   D. two–hour

第五节　介词

一、介词的定义和分类

（1）定义：介词又叫前置词，一般置于名词之前，只表示其后的名词或相当于名词的词与其他句子成分的关系。

（2）分类：按构成可以分为简单介词、复合介词和短语介词；介词按意义可以分为表示地点的介词、表示时间的介词、表示方式的介词、表示原因的介词等。

二、常见介词词义辨析

1. at, in, on（表示时间）

介词	用法	举例
at	多用于具体的钟点时刻前	at seven; at a quarter to one; at noon
in	表示一段时间，用于年、月、世纪、四季或泛指一天的上午、下午、晚上等	in the 21st century in spring/summer/autumn/winter in the morning/afternoon/evening in two days
on	用于表示具体某一天、星期几，某一天的早、中、晚或节日前	My cousin's birthday is on June 1st

2. since, from, for（表示时间段）

介词	用法	举例
since	指从某时一直延续至今，后接时间点，句子用完成时	He has lived here since 1993.
from	说明开始的时间，谓语可用过去、现在、将来的某种时态	From now on, I will learn English in the morning.
for	指动作延续贯穿了整个过程，后接时间段，句子用完成时	I have studied for nine years.

3. before, after, in（表示时间）

介词	用法	举例
before	在……之前	Test the heat of the water before getting in.
after	①表示以过去为起点的某一段时间之后可用于一般过去时。②与时间点连用表示过去或将来的某个时间之后	They finished the work after two years. I will ring you up after two o'clock.
in	指在一段时间之后，常用于将来时	He will go abroad in three days.

4. during, by, until（表示时间）

介词	用法	举例
during	"during+ 时间段"与延续性动词连用表示一段时间内的动作	He lives with his parents during these years.
by	"by+ 时间点"表示"到……为止"，如果 by 后面跟一个过去的时间点，句子的谓语动词要用过去完成时	We had learned 1,000 English words by the end of last term.
until	用在肯定句中，意为"直到……为止"，其前面的谓语动词要用延续性动词；用在否定句中，意为"直到……才"，其前面的谓语动词要用瞬间性动词	I waited for my mother until she came home. I didn't leave until my mother came home.

5. in, on, to（表示方位）

介词	用法	举例
in	表示在某一地区之内的某方位（属于该范围）	Fujian is in the southeast of China.
to	表示在某一地区之外的某方位（不属于该范围）	China is to the west of Japan.
on	表示与某地的毗邻关系	Hubei is on the north of Hunan.

6. on, over, above, under, below, beneath（表示方位）

介词	用法	举例
on	指在上面，表示两物体有接触面	There is a cup on the table.
over	在……的正上方，表示垂直在上	There is a bridge over the river.
above	指在上方，不一定表示正上方	Raise your arms above your head.
under	在……正下方，不确定两个物体是否有接触面	There are many bikes under the trees.
below	在……下方或低于……，不一定是垂直下方	The coat reaches below the knees.
beneath	在……下方，无间隔，有接触面	Beneath the blanket is grass.

7. in front of, in the front of, before（表示方位）

介词	用法	举例
in front of	表示"在……的前面"（范围外）	There are some trees in front of the classroom.
in the front of	表示"在……的前部"（范围内）	There is a teacher's desk in the front of the classroom.
before	所表示的位置关系和 in front of 相同，表示"在……前面"	He sits before me.

8. at, in, on（表示方位）

介词	用法	举例
at	与较小的地点连用	at the bus stop
in	与较大的地点连用	in China, in the world
on	表示在一个平面上	on the farm

9. by, with, in, through（表示方式）

介词	用法	举例
by	表示"用……方法、手段、途径等"或"乘坐（交通工具）"	The thief must have entered and left by the back door. He makes a living by selling newspapers.
with	表示"带着、伴随"，后面接具体有形的工具、身体部位、材料或其他行为方式	He plays table tennis with his left hand. He wrote these Chinese characters with a small bamboo stick.
in	表示"用……方式、材料、途径、语言"	He wrote many letters in English. You can do this in a different way.
through	表示"通过、凭借"	You can only achieve success through hard work.

10. about, on

介词	用法	举例
about	用于简单或浅显的论述，是一般用语	She told a story about Lei Feng.
on	多用于系统论述或专题演讲等，具有学术性	We're going to listen to a lecture on African history this afternoon.

11. except, but, besides, except for, apart from

介词	用法	举例
except/but	二者可互换使用，表示"除去、不包含"，强调"不包括在内"，一般表示同类之间的关系	They all passed the exam except/but Tom. She saw nothing except/but snow.
besides	表示"除了……还有"，强调"包含在内"。当 besides 和否定词连用时，可与 except, but 互换使用	Besides John, there will be five of us for dinner. She has no relatives besides/but/except an old aunt.
except for	表示"除……之外"，指对某种基本情况进行部分细节的修正，表示不同类之间的关系	Your composition is good except for several spelling mistakes. The road was empty except for a few cars.
apart from	可以和 except, but, besides, except for 互换使用	He had no one to take care of him apart from/besides/but/except his uncle.

12. across, through, over

介词	用法	举例
across	表示从表面通过，指从一端到另一端形成十字交叉穿过	The river was frozen, so they could go across the ice.
through	表示从物体中间穿过，通过的是三维空间	They hoped to walk through the forest before sunset.
over	表示越过、翻过	After they climbed over the hill, they found many flowers in the fields.

13. along, up, down

介词	用法	举例
along	表示沿着一条线平行行进	He walked along the road.
up	表示"从南到北、从地方到中央、从沿海到内地、从乡村到城市"等	She went up north for summer. Henry is up from the country.
down	表示"从北到南、从中央到地方、从内地到沿海、从城市到乡村"等	They have gone down to the country.
在不明确具体方向而只表示"沿路、街、巷"行进时，up 和 down 可互换使用，相当于 along		He saw an old man walking slowly along the road.

14. between, among

介词	用法	举例
between	"在……之间"，常指两者；当表示"两个以上之间"时，实际上仍指其中一个与其他中间一个之间的关系	The city lies between a river and hills. He has already known the difference between gases, solids and liquids.
among	"在……之间"，用于指三个或三个以上作为整体的人或物，通常表示"在同类中"	The Yangtze is among the longest rivers in the world. I was among the last persons to leave.

15. over, above, beyond

介词	用法	举例
over	可指数量、数目等的"多于""超过""……以上"	There's nothing in this shop above/over a dollar.
above	数量、数目、水平、年龄、温度等的"多于""超过""……以上"	Children above 3 years of age are ready for kindergarten. The temperature this summer is above normal.
beyond	"（范围）超过，为……所不及"	Einstein's special Theory of Relativity is quite beyond me. The beautiful scenes of Guilin are beyond description.

16. in, into

介词	用法	举例
in	通常表示位置（静态）	Is there any key in my purse?
into	表示动向，不表示目的地或位置	In April, I moved into her new flat.

17. on time, in time, in good time

介词短语	用法	举例
on time	意为"按时，准时"	The train pulled in on time.
in time	意为"及时、迟早"	They were just in time for the last train. In time you will forget him.
in good time	意为"尽早，提前"	Let me know in good time if you need any help.

18. at a time, at one time, at times

介词短语	用法	举例
at a time	意为"依次，每次"	Please come in one at a time, not all together.
at one time	意为"曾经，一度"，与一般过去时连用	They used to be good friends at one time.
at times	意为"有时，偶尔"，与一般现在时连用	I like Bob, but he's very annoying at times.

19. on the air, in the air

介词短语	用法	举例
on the air	意为"广播，发表广播演说的"	The president went on the air at 8 p.m. last night.
in the air	意为"在流传中，未确定的"	Rumors have been in the air. Our plans are still in the air.

20. in a way, in the way, on the way

介词短语	用法	举例
in a way	意为"在某种程度上"	In a way, we have already taken the first step.
in the way	意为"妨碍，使人不便"	I am afraid your car is in the way.
on the way	意为"在途中"	You had better be on the way soon.

21. in a word, in word, in words

介词短语	用法	举例
in a word	意为"总而言之"	In a word, he has tried his best.
in word	意为"表面，在口头上"	He is a friend in word only.
in words	意为"用语言"	She can't express her idea in words.

22. in turn, in return

介词短语	用法	举例
in turn	意为"依次,逐个地"或"转而,反过来"	The girls called out their names in turn. Theory is based on practice and in turn serves practice.
in return	意为"作为回报"	He gave her roses in return for her kindness.

23. out of question, out of the question

介词短语	用法	举例
out of question	意为"毋庸置疑"，一般作状语	He is out of question the best student in the class.
out of the question	意为"不值得讨论的，不可能的"，一般作表语	A new bicycle is out of the question—we can't afford it.

24. in the sun, under the sun

介词短语	用法	举例
in the sun	作状语，意为"在阳光下"	He sat in the sun reading a novel.
under the sun	用于加强语气，意为"天底下，在世界上""到底，究竟"	What under the sun did you mean? He is the last person under the sun that I want to see.

三、常见介词短语的含义

above all 最重要的是   above/over one's head 难以理解

at a loss 迷惑，茫然   at a price 以高价

at cost 按成本价   at first glance/sight 乍一看

at (one's)ease 放松，舒适   at hand 在手头，在附近，即将发生

at home 自由，无拘束   at least 至少

at most 至多   at one's convenience 方便时

at peace 平静   at random 随意，任意

at sea 在海上，茫然   at work 在工作

beyond words 难以言表   beyond/without doubt 无可怀疑

beyond description 难以形容   beyond/out of recognition 难以辨认

by chance/accident 偶然，意外地   by day/night 白天（夜间）

by hand 以手工，传递   by mistake 弄错

by request 应要求   by turns 轮流地，逐个地

for the time being 暂时   for fun 取乐，开玩笑

for good 永久，永远   for life 终身

for sale 待售   for short 简称，简写

for sure/certain 无疑   in addition 另外

in all 总共，总计   in brief/short 简而言之

in conclusion 最后   in debt 欠债

in essence 本质上   in fact 事实上

in fashion 流行，时髦   in general 一般来说

in order 妥当的，能用的   in other words 换言之

in part 部分地   in particular 尤其

in progress 进行中   in public 公开地，公然地

in secret 偷偷的，暗地的   in tears 流泪

in time 及时，迟早

in trouble　处于困境

in use 在使用中

in vain 徒劳的

on（the）average 平均

on business 因公

on display/show/view 在展示

on duty/watch　值班

on fire 着火

on guard 警戒

on hand 现有，随时可用

on holiday/vocation 在度假

on leave 在休假

on purpose 故意

on sale 出售，上市

on strike 在罢工

on the air 广播

on the contrary 相反

on the spot 当场，在现场

on the way 在途中

out of control/hand 失去控制

out of danger 脱险

out of date/fashion 过时，不流行

out of debt 不欠债

out of luck 不走运

out of necessity 出于必要

out of order 出故障，不正常

out of patience 不耐烦

out of pity 出于同情

out of sight 看不见

out of shape 变形，不健康

out of step 不一致

out of stock 缺货的

out of the ordinary 不正常，特殊

out of trouble 摆脱麻烦

out of work 失业

to one's advantage 对某人有利

to one's disappointment 使人失望

to one's face 当某人面

to one's joy 使人高兴

to one's regret 使人后悔

to one's relief 使人欣慰

to one's satisfaction 使人满意

to one's shame 使人惭愧

to one's surprise 使人吃惊

to some extent/degree 在某种程度上

under age 未成年

under attack 遭到攻击

under consideration 在考虑中

under construction　在建设中

under control 在控制中

under development 在研发中

under discussion 在讨论中

under examination 在审查中

under investigation 在调查中

under repair 在修理中

under treatment 在治疗中

under way 在进行中

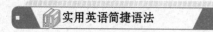
专项练习题

一、用适当的介词填空

1. My aunt arrived in Sydney _____ the night of January 2nd.

2. I began to learn to swim _____ the age of five.

3. I won't finish the work _____ night.

4. I have lived here _____ last September.

5. They had built a new bridge _____ the end of last year.

6. They had a big party _____ Christmas Eve.

7. I usually play basketball with my friends _____ Friday afternoon.

8. I have learnt English _____ ten years.

9. I saw the movie _____ the end of last month.

10. My brother will be back from Australia _____ a few days.

11. My father has worked in this hospital _____ twenty years ago.

12. We had a great time _____ the party.

13. I had a pain _____ my leg this morning.

14. There are many trees _____ both sides of the street.

15. Turn right _____ the second crossing.

16. I have read the news _____ the newspaper.

17. He cut down the trees _____ an axe.

18. She wrote the letter _____ French.

19. He passed the examination _____ hard work.

20. He makes a living _____ writing novels.

21. The tool was made _____ hand.

22. Everyone is surprised _____ that piece of surprising news.

23. She usually goes to work _____ her bike when it rains.

24. His composition is good, _____ some spelling mistakes.

25. There are other visitors _____ me.

26. She discovered the problem _____ accident.

27. He suffered _____ poor eyesight and could no longer read properly.

28. She works _____ a secretary for a big company.

29. Are there any good films _____ at the cinema this week?

30. Smith and his family are away ____ holiday.

二、单项选择

1. This kind of wine is made ____ grapes.
    A. up of   B. into
    C. by   D. from

2. Wood can be made ____ chairs and tables.
    A. of   B. for
    C. out   D. into

3. ____ our surprise, the twin sisters went to Peking University at the same time last year.
    A. With   B. In
    C. To   D. By

4. Japan lies ____ the east of Asia and ____ the east of China.
    A. in, on   B. in, to
    C. to, on   D. on, to

5. We couldn't finish our work so early ____ your help.
    A. without   B. with
    C. for   D. by

6. We can get fresh water from rain, from rivers, or from ____ the ground.
    A. across   B. under
    C. over   D. off

7. A typhoon has been ____ its way. Please come home as quickly as possible.
    A. on   B. in
    C. by   D. at

8. What a nice day! We should go sightseeing ____ watching TV in the hotel.
    A. because of   B. instead of
    C. together with   D. out of

9. If success is a gate, the road ____ it must be made up of difficulties.
    A. against   B. opposite
    C. towards   D. near

10. The university student borrowed some money ____ his friends to start his own business.
    A. from   B. onto

C. at   D. in

11. Please give me some advice ____ how to learn English.

A. in   B. on

C. about   D. off

12. He has got ____ the habit ____ listening to the news broadcast at 6:30 every morning.

A. in, of   B. into, for

C. into, of   D. /, of

13. ____ his leg broken, he wouldn't come to school as usual.

A. As   B. With

C. For   D. since

14. Mary shares a bedroom ____ her sister.

A. with   B. and

C. to   D. together

15. We can see a playground ____ the two tall building.

A. between   B. among

C. in   D. at

16. Let me introduce you ____ my friend.

A. with   B. by

C. for   D. to

17. I live ____ the market. So I have to drive to buy vegetables and fruits.

A. far away   B. near to

C. far from   D. near

18. We'll hold a party in celebration of the 10th birthday of our company ____ Friday.

A. in   B. on

C. at   D. for

19. It is very important ____ people to have food and water every day.

A. for   B. of

C. with   D. about

20. I don't know how to begin a talk with Betty. She can sit all day long ____ a word.

A. by   B. with

C. in   D. without

21. How long did it take you to swim ____ the river.

    A. over   B. across

    C. through   D. above

22. I like flowers. I hope to study at a school ____ many flowers and trees in it.

    A. in   B. with

    C. on   D. by

23. TV is short ____ television.

    A. with   B. of

    C. for   D. at

24. A teacher is often compared ____ a candle.

    A. with   B. to

    C. at   D. at

25. They met ____ accident, so they didn't know each other well.

    A. from   B. on

    C. by   D. of

26. Bonnie looks very smart and is always ____ pink, because pink is her favorite color.

    A. with   B. on

    C. about   D. in

27. My house is ____ the other side of the street.

    A. on   B. in

    C. by   D. to

28. Books are made ____ paper while paper is mainly made ____ wood.

    A. of, of   B. from, from

    C. of, from   D. from, of

29. I wrote ____ my brother last Sunday, but I haven't heard ____ him up to now.

    A. from, to   B. to, of

    C. to, to   D. to, from

30. The moon light goes ____ the window and makes the room bright.

    A. across   B. through

    C. over   D. in

31. ——Let's get the key ____ the question?

    ——OK. Let's start.

    A. For   B. with

C. on   D. to

32. Every one of you is looking forward ____ getting a good result. Better think carefully before writing down your answers. Wish you success!

    A. on   B. in

    C. to   D. at

33. In this class one student ____ five is a league member.

    A. from   B. in

    C. of   D. under

34. If you get on well ____ your classmates, you'll enjoy your school life more.

    A. to   B. at

    C. with   D. in

35. We agree ____ their suggestion.

    A. to   B. with

    C. on   D. in

36. ____ a terrible rainy night, many farmers' houses were destroyed.

    A. In   B. On

    C. at   D. to

37. You can't mix oil ____ water.

    A. up   B. of

    C. by   D. with

38. It's very kind ____ you. Thank you for your help.

    A. of   B. for

    C. to   D. on

39. There is a picture ____ my family on the wall.

    A. of   B. up

    C. after   D. to

40. ——Is the film interesting?

    —— thought it would be. But ____, it's very boring.

    A. in all   B. in fact

    C. in addition   D. in future

第六节 形容词和副词

一、形容词的定义和分类

（一）定义：形容词是用于修饰名词、表示人或事物特征或性质的词

（二）分类

分类方式	分类名称	特征	举例
构成	简单形容词	由一个单词构成	easy, honest, good, useful, sunny, friendly…
	复合形容词	由两个或两个以上的单词构成	sea-sick, snow-covered, peace-loving, hard-working, narrow-minded, duty-free, short-sighted, good-looking, ever-green, ten-metre-deep, all-round…
意义	静态形容词	描绘人或物的静态特征	short, small, deep, ugly, beautiful…
	动态形容词	带有动作含义的形容词	witty, patient, generous, shy, naughty, noisy…

二、形容词的语法功能

（一）形容词在句中可作定语、表语、宾语补足语、状语，有时也作主语或宾语

1. 用于名词前作定语，当修饰不定代词时，放在不定代词后

It is a beautiful flower.

Someone else has done it.

2. 放在系动词后作表语

常见的后面跟形容词作表语的动词：

（1）become, come, fall, get, go, grow, make, turn（表示"变成某种状态"）。

The leaves turn yellow in autumn.

（2）continue, hold, keep, lie, remain, stay（表示"保持某种状态"）。

It's going to stay cold for some time.

（3）appear, feel, look, smell, sound, taste（表示"感觉"）。

The beer tastes very delicious.

3. 作宾语补足语

The news made her very excited.

4. 作状语

He came back (being) disappointed and exhausted. （伴随状语）

(Although) Young in years, he is old in experience. （让步状语）

5. 作主语、宾语

Young and old joined in the discussion.

The old always think of old things.

（二）形容词作定语时后置的情况

修饰不定代词时，放在其后	No one else can solve the problem.
形容词短语作定语时，放在名词之后	Have you found a person (that/who is) suitable for the job? That is a hall (which is) eight meters long and seven meters wide.
表语形容词作定语时，放在名词之后。这类形容词包括：ill, asleep, awake, alone, alive, aware, afraid, alike, available 等	He is the most famous scientist alive. Time alone will show who was right.
和空间、时间、单位连用时	There is a bridge 50 meters long.
以 –able/–ible 结尾的形容词可置于最高级或 only 修饰的名词之后	the best book available the only solution possible

（三）多个形容词作前置定语时，按与名词的关系密切程度，排序如下

描述→尺寸→新旧（年龄）→形状→颜色→产地→材料→用途 + 名词

a small old round table（尺寸→新旧→形状 + 名词）

a dirty old blue shirt（描述→新旧→颜色 + 名词）

a beautiful large green Chinese carpet（描述→尺寸→颜色→产地 + 名词）

a round brown wooden table（形状→颜色→材料 + 名词）

a valuable old French writing desk（描述→新旧→产地→用途 + 名词）

三、副词的定义和分类

（一）定义：是用来修饰动词、形容词、副词、介词短语或整个句子的词

（二）分类：

时间副词	表示时间的 today, tomorrow, already, early, soon, just, still, yet, before, later...
地点副词	表示方位和方向的 ahead, below, upstairs, here, up, left...
频度副词	例如：twice, monthly, always, frequently, often, sometimes, rarely, ever, never...

方式副词	例如：slowly, warmly, quickly, suddenly…
程度副词	例如：almost, too, enough, fairly, quite, hardly, very, even, just, only…
疑问副词	引导特殊疑问句或名词性从句，如：when, where, why, how…
连接副词	表示上下文逻辑关系，如：however, moreover, therefore, otherwise…
关系副词	引导定语从句，如：when, where, why…
观点副词	表示说话人对自己说话的态度，如：honestly, personally, actually, indeed, maybe…

四、副词的语法功能

（一）副词在句中多作状语，有时也可作表语、定语、介词宾语等

1. 作状语，可修饰动词、形容词、副词、介词短语或整个句子；修饰名词时，用来加强语气

She left shortly after the meeting.

Frankly, I don't agree with you.

副词作状语时在句中的位置一般如下：

时间副词	一般放句首或句尾。（early, late, before, later, yet 等一般放在句尾，already, just 一般放在动词前面）	We will visit the Summer Palace later. They have already been to the Canada twice.
地点副词	一般放在动词之后，但 here, there 还可以放在句首	We had a meeting here yesterday. Here we had a meeting yesterday.
频度副词	一般放在 be 动词后或助动词与主要动词之间，但 sometimes, often 等还可放在句首或句尾；usually 可放在句首；once 可放在句尾；twice, three times 等一般放在句尾	Sometimes I get up late. The manager always has lunch at the office. Take this medicine three times a week.
方式副词	一般放在行为动词之后，suddenly 放在句首、句尾或动词之前	He never runs as quickly as a car. Suddenly he saw a light in the dark cave.
程度副词	可放在所修饰词的前面或后面	She is much pleased by his words. I don't know him well.
疑问副词	用于对句子的状语进行提问，位置总是在句首	When and where were you born? Why did little Edison sit on some eggs?
连接副词	用来引导主语从句、宾语从句和表语从句，在从句中作状语	That is why everyone is afraid of him. He wondered how he could do it.
关系副词	用来引导定语从句，在从句中作状语	This is the place where Mr. Zhou once lived.

2. 作表语，主要有表示方位的 above, across, inside, upstairs 等，表示方向的 up, down, on, in, off, out, away 等

Time is up.

I must be off now.

3. 作定语，通常放在被修饰词的后面

I saw him the week before.

I met her on my way home.

4. 作介词的宾语

She looked everywhere but/except there.

（二）多个副词作状语的排列次序

如果一个句子中有两个或两个以上的状语时，可遵循以下原则：

1. 方式状语→地点状语→时间状语

They are studying hard at college now.

She spoke very well at the meeting last night.

2. 具体的状语→笼统的状语（小的状语→大的状语）

I saw him at 5 o'clock yesterday evening.

They ate in a little restaurant in town.

3. run/go/drive+ 地点状语→方式状语→时间状语

He went to the hospital hurriedly at night.

（三） 在以 be 动词、助动词（情态动词）结尾的句子中，often, never, seldom, just, really, actually, always, almost, still 等副词要放在 be 动词、助动词（情态动词）的前面

He is often late for class, but she seldom is.

He has already finished the job. —He already has.

She still worked in the lab. —She still did.

五、形容词和副词的比较级、最高级

（一）形容词比较级和最高级的变化规则

1. 一般情况下加 er/est

tall → taller/tallest　　short → shorter/shortest　　quick → quicker/quickest

2. 以不发音的 e 结尾加 r/st

nice → nicer/nicest　　large → larger/largest　　fine → finer/finest

3. 双写尾字母加 er/est（※ 记忆小窍门：大、热、胖、瘦、湿、悲伤）

big → bigger/biggest　hot → hotter/hottest　fat → fatter/fattest

thin → thinner/thinnest　wet → wetter/wettest　sad → sadder/saddest

4. 以辅音字母加 y 结尾，变 y 为 i 加 er/est

happy → happier/happiest　　lucky → luckier/luckiest

5. 多音节（三个或三个以上音节）形容词和少数双音节形容词前面加 more/most

more/most interesting　　　more/most difficult

more/most beautiful　　　more/most tired

6. 形容词比较级和最高级的特殊形式

（1）many/much → more/most。

（2）little → less/least（修饰不可数名词）。

（3）few → fewer/fewest（修饰可数名词）。

（4）good/well → better/best。

（5）bad/ill → worse/worst。

（6）far → farther/farthest

　　　→ further/furthest。

（7）old → older/oldest（旧的、老的、年长的）用于含比较含义的句子中

　　　→ elder/eldest（老的、年长的）　elder brother/son。

（二）副词比较级和最高级的变化规则

1. 一般情况下加 er/est

fast → faster → fastest　　　hard → harder → hardest

He studied harder than Peter.

He runs（the）fastest in his class.

2. 以不发音的 e 结尾加 r/st

late → later → latest

3. 以辅音字母加 y 结尾的，变 y 为 i 加 er/est

early → earlier → earliest

4. 以 ly 结尾的方式副词，通常在前面加 more/most

slowly → more slowly → most slowly

quickly → more quickly → most quickly

5. 特殊形式

well → better/best　　　　badly → worse/worst

much → more/most　　　　little → less/least

（三）形容词和副词比较级的常见应用结构

1. A… 比较级 +than…B

My father is older than my mother.

The weather in Shanghai is better than that in Wuhan.

Tom drives more carefully than John.

※ 比较的 B 如果是人称代词，常用宾格。

He is taller than me.

如果比较的 A 和 B 是同类事物，则 B 可用 this/that one，如为复数，则 B 用 these/those。

This dress is more beautiful than that one.

These dresses are more beautiful than those.

2. 反向比较："not + 比较级 + than" "not as/so…as" 或 "less… + than"

This chapter is not more difficult than that one.

This chapter is not so/as difficult as that one.

This chapter is less difficult than that one.

3. Which/Who + be + 比较级 , A or B?

Who is taller, Peter or Mary?

Which car runs faster, the black one or the red one?

4. 比较级 + and + 比较级 / more and more + 原级（"越来越……"）

It is getting colder and colder.

She is becoming more and more interested in English.

It rained more and more heavily.

5. the + 比较级……， the + 比较级……（"越……，就越……"）

The easier, the better. 越容易越好。

The more trees we plant, the less air pollution will be.

The more we smile, the happier we will feel.

The faster I type, the more mistakes I make.

6. 在 "of the two……" 结构中，用 "the + 形容词比较级"

Of the two boys, Bob is the stronger.

She behaves（the）more politely of the two girls.

7. ……数词 + year（s）+ older/younger + than… [……比……大 / 小……（岁）]

Peter is three years older than Mary.

Mary is three years younger than Peter.

（四）形容词和副词最高级的常见应用结构

1. …the + 形容词最高级 + 范围（in our class, of the three, I have ever done…）

It is the largest room in our school.

My father is the fattest in my family.

Of all the students in his class, Tom made the fewest mistakes in his composition.

Of all the girls in my class, she studies（the）hardest.

2. Which/Who…the + 最高级，A, B or C?

Which is the fastest, the bike, the car or the train?

3. 如果形容词最高级前有形容词性物主代词、名词所有格、序数词等修饰，则 the 省略

This is my best pen.

Playing tennis is her latest hobby.

4. the + 序数词 + 最高级

the second tallest　　the third longest　　the fifth biggest

5. one of the + 形容词最高级 + 复数名词

In my opinion, Suzhou is one of the most beautiful cities in China.

6. 形容词最高级 most 前不加定冠词或加不定冠词时，不表示比较，相当于 very

This is a most beautiful flower.

The book you lent me last week was most dull.

7. 同一范围内形容词比较级与最高级的转换

Peter is the strongest student in our class.

=Peter is stronger than all the other students in our class.

=Peter is stronger than any other student in our class.

（五）常见可修饰形容词比较级和最高级的副词

1. 常见的可以修饰形容词比较级的副词有：much, far, a lot, rather, a little, a bit, slightly, even, any, yet 和 no 等

This book is far more interesting than that one.

It was a bit more entertaining than the last play we saw.

2. 常见的可以修饰形容词最高级的副词有：much, by far, quite, nearly 和 easily 等

The last of these reasons is by far the most important.

She's quite the most amazing person I've ever met.

六、形容词和副词的原级比较

（一）...as+ 形容词原级 +as...

Lucy is as beautiful as Mary.

（二）...not+as/so+ 形容词原级 +as... /...less+ 形容词原级 +than...

This book is not as interesting as that one.

This book is less interesting than that one.

（三）... 实义动词 +as+ 副词原级 +as...

Lucy sings as beautifully as Mary.

（四）...as+ 形容词原级 + 名词 +as...

There are as many students in Class One as in Class Two.

There is as much snow this year as last year.

（五）在原级比较结构前可加 just, quite, almost, nearly, half, twice, three times, one third 等程度状语进行修饰

It is quite/just/almost/nearly as cold as yesterday.

This room is three times/half/one third as large as that one.

（六）当"as+ 原级 +as"与表示重量、数量、时间、距离、价格等名词连用时，往往不表示比较，而是构成一个形容词或副词短语，意为"重达……，多达……，高达……"等

The river is as deep as 10 meters.

As many as 100 people were injured in the accident.

The book was written as early as the sixth century.

> 知识点拓展（一）

1. farther/farthest 与 further/furthest 的区别

（1）表示距离时，均意为"远"，可互换。

I'm so tired that I can't go any farther/further.

（2）表示抽象概念时，意为"进一步，更多的"，只能用 further/furthest。

She went abroad for further study.

2. older/oldest 与 elder/eldest 的区别

（1）older/oldest 意为"年龄大的"，可指人，也可指物，作定语或表语，可用于

---

than 引导的比较状语从句。

（2）elder/eldest 意为"年长的"，仅指人，作定语修饰名词。

My elder brother is 7 years older than me.

> ➤ 知识点拓展（二）

有些副词具有两种形式：一种与形容词同形，表示具体意义；另一种是形容词后加后缀 –ly，表示抽象或引申意义。

high（高高地，在或向高处）	→	highly（极，非常）
hard（猛烈地，努力地）	→	hardly（几乎不）
late（晚、迟）	→	lately（最近）
close（靠近）	→	closely（细心地，严密地）
dead（完全地，极其）	→	deadly（非常，死一般地）
wide（宽阔地，完全地）	→	widely（广泛地，很大地）
near（接近地，附近地）	→	nearly（几乎，差不多）
deep（表示具体深度）	→	deeply（表示抽象深度，深深地）
most（最，很）	→	mostly（主要地，大多数地）
just（只是，刚刚，正好）	→	justly（公正地）
full（直接地，正好）	→	fully（完全地，彻底地）

> ➤ 知识点拓展（三）

表示"最高程度"的形容词没有比较级和最高级，例如：

favorite, excellent, extreme, perfect, superior, inferior, senior, junior, former, latter, preferable, absolute, adequate, foremost, last, parallel, supreme, utmost.

He is superior to the other students in his class.（√）

He is more superior to the other boys in his class.（×）

专项练习题

一、用所给单词的适当形式填空

1. He arrives at the bus station an hour ＿＿＿（early）than yesterday.

2. Today is ＿＿＿（wet）day in August.

3. I live far from my school, Mary lives much ＿＿＿, but Bob lives the ＿＿＿.（far）

4. He hopes to provide a more comfortable and _____ (wealth) life for his children.

5. My _____ brother is four years _____ than me. (old)

6. Who is the _____ (good) in Physics in your class?

7. Tom is the _____ (tall) of the two boys.

8. The Yellow River is the second _____ (long) river in China.

9. All the movie theatres are good, but this one has _____ (comfortable) seats.

10. He is not so _____ (strong) as him.

二、单项选择题

1. Jogging is _____ than many sports——to start, just get some comfortable sports clothes and good running shoes.

    A. cheap   B. cheaper

    C. cheapest   D. the cheapest

2. Mike lives _____ from school of all the students, so he always takes a bus to school.

    A. far   B. farther

    C. further   D. the farthest

3. ——You have made great progress on your study.

    ——Thank you. I believe _____ you work, the better grades you will get.

    A. the worse   B. the harder

    C. the more careless   D. the more careful

4. I think science is _____ than Japanese.

    A. much important   B. important

    C. much more important   D. more much important

5. ——What do you think of Tom's speaking?

    ——No one does _____ in our class.

    A. good   B. better

    C. well   D. best

6. ——Which month has _____ days in a year?

    ——February.

    A. few   B. little

    C. the least   D. the fewest

7. _____ the temperature, _____ water turns into steam.

    A. The high; the fast   B. Higher; faster

    C. The more higher; faster   D. The higher; the faster

8. ——There used to be lots of fish in the lake.

——Yes, but there are very_____ now.

　　A. few   B. fewer

　　C. little   D. less

9. Nancy and Lucy are twins. In some way they look the same, but Nancy is _____ than Lucy.

　　A. tall   B. taller

　　C. tallest   D. the taller

10. Which sport do you like _____ , swimming, running or shooting?

　　A. well   B. better

　　C. best   D. the best

11. In the piano contest, my brother didn't play well and I did _____.

　　A. very well   B. much better

　　C. very good   D. even worse

12. He made the _____ mistakes in the dictation.

　　A. less   B. least

　　C. fewer   D. fewest

13. They have just cleaned the windows, so the room looks_____.

　　A. brightest   B. least bright

　　C. less bright   D. much brighter

14. The actress is already 50, but she looks _____ than she really is.

　　A. young   B. more young

　　C. more younger   D. much younger

15. ——Which city has _____ population, Shanghai, Hong Kong or Qingdao?

——Shanghai, of course.

　　A. the smallest   B. the least

　　C. the most   D. the largest

16. Of the two coats, she'd like to choose the _____ one to save money for a book.

　　A. cheapest   B. cheaper

　　C. more expensive   D. most expensive

17. He knows _____ about computers than me.

　　A. much   B. more

　　C. most   D. many

18. John plays football _____, if not better than, David.

　　A. as well   B. as well as

C. so well   D. so well a

19. If we had followed his plan, we could have done the job better with _____ money and_____ people.

    A. less; less   B. fewer; fewer

    C. less; fewer   D. fewer; less

20. Some Chinese singers sing English songs just as _____ as native speakers do.

    A. good   B. better

    C. well   D. best

21. On the river there is _____ bridge.

    A. an old stone fine   B. an fine old stone

    C. an old fine stone   D. a fine old stone

22. There are _____ chairs in the living–room.

    A. dark three very comfortable blue   B. three very dark comfortable blue

    C. three very comfortable dark blue   D. very comfortable three dark blue

23. The doctor said that there was _____ with the injured child.

    A. nothing serious wrong   B. seriously wrong nothing

    C. nothing seriously wrong   D. serious nothing wrong

24. The black pen is much _____ expensive than the red one.

    A. too   B. less

    C. fewer   D. lower

25. He eats _____.

    A. twice as the amount as you   B. twice the amount that you eat

    C. twice as more as you   D. twice as most as you eat

26. Lu Xun is _____ the most famous writer in China.

    A. by far   B. still far

    C. even far   D. much more

27. _____, the better I feel.

    A. When I take more exercise   B. Taking more exercise

    C. The more exercise I take   D. The more I take exercise

28. His salary as a barber is much higher _____.

    A. in comparison with a teacher's   B. than that of a teacher

    C. than a teacher   D. than of a teacher's

29. I found her becoming _____.

    A. more nervous and more nervous   B. most and most nervous

C. more and more nervous　　　　D. nervous and nervous

30. The scientists want to know about the sea life____.

A. deep in ocean　　　　B. deeply in the ocean

C. deep in the ocean　　　　D. in the ocean deeply

 第七节 动词和动词短语

一、动词的定义和分类

（一）定义：表示动作或状态的词

（二）分类：根据在句子中的功能，动词可以分为以下四类

分类依据	名称	特征	例词
按意义和句法功能	实义动词	本身意义完整，能够独立作谓语	study, enjoy, eat, wash…
	助动词	本身无词义或意义不完整，不能单独作谓语，须与其他动词连用，帮助构成各种时态、语态、否定句或疑问句	be, have/has, do/does/did, will, shall
	系动词	本身有意义，但不能单独作谓语，需和表语一起构成系表结构	be, become, get, turn, grow, keep, remain, seem, ,look, sound, smell, taste, feel
	情态动词	表示"能力、允许、必要、禁止、意愿、可能"等情感或态度的动词。词义不完整，不能单独作谓语，和实义动词一起构成谓语，多无人称和数的变化	can, could, may, might, must, need, ought to, should, will, would, dare
按照与主语的关系	谓语动词	在句中作谓语，可与助动词和情态动词连用，也可单独使用，但必须与主语在人称和数上保持一致	study, enjoy, eat, wash 等实义动词
	非谓语动词	在句中不起谓语作用，可担当主语、宾语、表语、定语、状语等，在人称和数上不受主语的制约	to do, doing, done

二、助动词

　　助动词不能独立使用，须与其他动词连用，帮助实义动词构成不同的时态和语态，表达不同的意义。常见的助动词有：be, do/does/did, have/has, shall, will 等。

　　1. be 的用法

　　（1）与动词的现在分词构成各种进行时态。

I am playing computer games.

The children have been watching TV all morning.

（2）与动词的过去分词构成被动语态。

The book was written in English.

The book has been translated into many languages.

2. do/does/did 的用法

（1）在一般现在时和一般过去时中，构成否定或疑问结构，或构成祈使句。

She doesn't speak English.

Did you see him in the library?

Don't be so nervous!

（2）用于加强语气，意为"一定，务必，的确"。

Do come to the party tomorrow evening.

I did go, but she wasn't in.

3. have/has/had 的用法

（1）与动词的过去分词构成完成时态。

He has just left.

Have you ever been to the Great Wall?

They had got everything ready before I came.

（2）had 用于虚拟语气。

If you had posted the letter, Mother would have received it last Monday.

Had I left earlier, I wouldn't have missed the train.

4. will 和 shall 的用法

助动词 shall 和 will 和动词原形构成将来时。shall/should 仅限于第一人称，will/would 可用于所有人称。shall/should 和 will/would 也可用作情态动词。

Will you stay here a little longer?

I shall go to Hong Kong next week.

He told me that he would see me off at the station.

三、系动词

系动词不能单独用作谓语，后边必须跟表语（亦称补语），构成系表结构说明主语的状况、性质、特征等情况。

分类	系动词	用法	例句
状态系动词	be	表示"是"	He is a teacher.
持续系动词	keep, rest, remain, stay, lie, stand	表示主语继续或保持一种状况或态度	He always kept silent at meeting.
表象系动词	seem, appear	表示"看起来像"这一概念	He seems / (to be) very sad.
感官系动词	feel, look, smell, sound, taste	与五种感官相关的动词	The flower smells very sweet.
变化系动词	become, grow, turn, fall, get, go come, run	表示主语变成另一种状态	He became mad after that.
终止系动词	prove（证实）, turn out（变成、结果是）	表示主语已终止动作	The rumor proved false.

【注意】有些动词既可以作系动词，又可以作行为动词，如 grow, get, turn, look, feel, smell, sound, taste 等。用 be 替换句子中的这些动词，如果句子仍然成立，被替换掉的就是系动词，反之就是行为动词。

变化系动词	go	后面接形容词多表示"（从好的状态）变成坏的状态"；go 后面的表语为 mad，crazy，blind，lame 或表示颜色的形容词时，go 前面的主语一般为人	In hot weather, meat goes bad. He went mad last year.
	grow	后面可以接表示人或物的特征的静态形容词，也可以接表示天气的形容词。侧重于"逐渐变成某种状态"	The girl grew thinner and thinner.
	turn	后面多接表示颜色或天气的形容词。侧重于"变得与以前完全不同"	The man turned blue with fear.
	get	"get+ 形容词"多用在口语中。get 能替代 become，但 become 较为正式。get 与 become 前面的主语既可以是人也可以是物	His coat has become/got badly torn.

【注意】系动词 become、turn、get、go 后面可加名词作表语，其他的"变成"类系动词后面不能跟名词作表语。

His dream has become a reality.

四、实义动词

实义动词又称行为动词，指具有实际意义的动词，例如：swim, eat, take 等，可以单独作谓语。

（一）根据动词能否直接跟宾语，分为及物动词、不及物动词。

1. 及物动词：后面必须带宾语，有些及物动词可以带双宾语或宾语补足语

I believe that the committee will consider our suggestion.

The judge proved him innocent.

2. 不及物动词：本身意义完整，后面不用跟宾语

My head ached.

Leaves fall when fall comes.

3. 有些动词可以兼作及物动词和不及物动词。这样的词分为两种情况

①兼作及物动词和不及物动词时，意义不变。

When did you leave?

They left Shanghai last week.

②兼作及物动词和不及物动词时，意义改变。

She couldn't stand the cold.

Don't stand in the rain.

【注意】不及物动词有时可加副词或介词，构成短语动词，相当于及物动词。大部分及物动词有被动语态，不及物动词没有被动语态形式，要用主动表示被动。

Everyone listened to the lecture with great interest.

The door locks tightly.

（二）延续性动词和非延续性动词

（1）延续性动词：表示各种持续的活动，如：walk, sleep, work, do, play, run, rain, wait, read 等，可用于进行时态。

The boys are playing football on the playground.

It has been raining the whole morning.

（2）非延续性动词：又称瞬间性动词，表示短暂的动作，没有持续性，如：open, knock, begin, join, marry, go, come, arrive, leave, become, get, turn, grow 等，一般不能与表示一段时间的状语连用。

Someone is knocking at the door.

The old man has died.

The leaves are turning yellow.

五、常见实义动词词义辨析

1. get, reach, arrive（三个"到达"）

（1）get to+ 地点名词。

（2）reach，及物动词，后面可直接加地点名词。

（3）arrive in+ 大地点（名词），arrive at+ 小地点（名词）。

2. borrow, lend, keep（三个"借"）

（1）borrow，非延续性动词，表示"借入"，搭配：borrow sth. from sb.

（2）lend，非延续性动词，表示"借出"，搭配：lend sth. to sb.

3. join, take part in, attend（三个"参加"）

（1）join，一般指加入"党派"或"组织"，如参军、入党等。

（2）take part in，指参加聚会或活动。

（3）attend，一般指出席会议。

4. dress, put on, wear（三个"穿"）

（1）dress，dress sb. 给某人穿衣服；dress sb. up 装扮某人。

（2）put on，穿上、戴上，表示动作。

（3）wear，穿着、戴着，表示状态。

5. see, look, watch, read（四个"看"）

（1）see，看见，表示结果。

（2）look，看，表示动作，不及物动词，后面需要加介词才能跟宾语。

（3）watch，观看（比赛、电视等）。

（4）read，看（书、报），表示阅读。

6. bring, take, carry, fetch（四个"拿"）

（1）bring，带来，拿来，表示"拿到靠近说话人的地方"。

（2）take，拿去，带走，表示"拿到远离说话人的地方"。

（3）carry，提、拿、搬，多指用力移动，没有方向。

（4）fetch，去取，去拿，表示"往返拿东西"。

7. speak, say, talk, tell（四个"说"）

（1）speak，作及物动词时后面常接表示语言的名词。

（2）say，常跟直接引语和间接引语，且表示说话的内容。

（3）talk，不及物动词，常跟介词 to 和 with 连用，意为"和……谈话"，也表示具有说话的能力。

（4）tell，意为"告诉"，当与 story 连用时，意为"讲故事"。

8. spend, cost, take, pay（四个"花费"）

（1）spend，人作主语，表花费时间或金钱，spend on sth. /spend（in）doing sth.

（2）cost，物作主语，表示"某物花费多少钱"。

（3）take，可用于固定句型，It takes/took + 一段时间 + to do sth.，意为"花费一段时间做某事"。

（4）pay，指花费金钱，多与介词 for 连用。

9. lose, fail, beat, win（四个"输赢"）

（1）lose，意为"输"，常用搭配为：lose to sb.。

（2）fail，意为"失败"或"未做成某事"。

（3）beat，意为"打败"，后接"打败的对象"。

（4）win，意为"赢得"，后接"荣誉、地位、比赛"等。

10. look for, find（两个"找"）

（1）look for，强调寻找的过程。

（2）find，强调找的结果。

11. listen to, hear（两个"听"）

（1）listen to，强调听的过程。

（2）hear，强调听的结果。

12. assure, ensure, insure

（1）assure 意为"使相信"。

He assured us of his ability to solve the problem.

I can assure you that the medicine is perfectly safe.

（2）ensure 意为"确保，保证"。

This book ensured his success.

These pills will ensure you a good night's sleep.

（3）insure 和 ensure 实际上是一个词，但 insure 还有"保险"的意思。

She has insured her life.

She insured the house for 2,000 dollars.

13. adapt, adopt

（1）adapt 意为"适应，改写"。

Our eyes slowly adapted to the dark.

Three of her novels have been adapted for TV plays.

（2）adopt 意为"采纳，接受""收养"。

We adopted his production method.

Having no children of their own, they decided to adopt an orphan.

14. damage, ruin, destroy, spoil

（1）damage "损害，损坏"，含可修补、弥补的意思。ruin 的毁坏程度强于 damage。

The building was damaged/ruined by the fire.

Smoking can damage/ruin your health.

（2）spoil "破坏，糟蹋"，含失去完美性的意思，语气弱于 ruin。另外 spoil 还有"宠坏"的意思。

The bad news has spoiled/ruined my day.

She spoils those kids of hers.

（3）destroy "摧毁"，指彻底毁掉，无法恢复，也可以指希望、计划等破灭。

The bomb destroyed the whole building.

His hope of being a writer was destroyed.

15. hurt, injure, wound

（1）hurt 和 injure 同义，指在某次意外的事故或事件中 "受伤"，多用于被动语态。

He was badly hurt/injured in the accident.

Did you hurt/injure yourself?

（2）wound 多指在战争中 "受伤"，如刀伤或枪伤等。

The bullet wounded him in the shoulder.

Ten soldiers were killed and thirty were seriously wounded.

（3）hurt 和 wound 还可以表示对某人感情的伤害。

What he said hurt/wounded me deeply.

He was so hurt/wounded that he could not say a word.

16. treat, cure, heal

（1）treat 意为 "治疗"，指医治的过程。

Last year the hospital treated forty cases of liver cancer.

Some skin diseases are difficult to treat.

（2）cure 意为 "治愈"，指医治的结果。

The doctor cured her of lung cancer.

This illness cannot be cured easily.

（3）heal 意为 "康复"，指伤口或烧伤愈合。

The wound healed slowly.

The wound is not yet healed.

17. lie, lay

原形	过去式	过去分词	现在分词	词性	词义
Lie	lay	Lain	lying	不及物动词	躺，位于
	lied	Lied	lying	不及物动词	说谎
Lay	laid	Laid	laying	及物动词	放置，产卵

There is a book lying on the table.

The university lies in the east of the city.

She lied（to them）about her age to get the job.

He laid his coat over the chair.

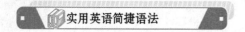

The cuckoo lays its eggs in other birds' nests.

18. arise, rise, arouse, raise

原 形	过去式	过去分词	现在分词	词性	词义
arise	Arose	arisen	arising	不及物动词	出现
rise	Rose	risen	rising	不及物动词	上升，起身
arouse	Aroused	aroused	arousing	及物动词	唤醒，引起
raise	Raised	raised	raising	及物动词	举起，提高

Some unexpected difficulties have arisen.

He rose to welcome me.

Her behavior aroused the suspicions of the police.

Raise your hand if you have any questions.

六、常见动词短语

take 短语		get 短语	
take up 占据		get to 到达	
take away 带走、拿走		get up 起床	
take off 起飞、脱掉		get over 克服	
take down 写下、记下		get on 进展	
take place 发生		get off 离开	
take care of 照顾		get together 相聚	
take part in 参加		Get ready for 为……做准备	
turn 短语		keep 短语	
turn on 打开		keep out 留在外面	
turn off 关闭		keep off 使……不接近	
turn up 开大、调高		keep up with 并驾齐驱	
turn down 调低、关小		keep away from 远离	
turn in 上交		keep in touch 保持联系	
turn out 结果是		keep healthy 保持健康	

续表

make 短语	make a decision 做出决定	come 短语	come on 加油、快点
	make a mistake 犯错		come out 出现、出版
	make a living 谋生		come over 短暂造访
	make up 组成、构成		come along 出现
go 短语	go on 继续	look 短语	look at 看
	go back 回到		look for 寻找
	go away 走开、离开		look after 照顾
	go by（时间）流逝		look up 查阅
	go over 仔细检查		look through 浏览
	go off 爆炸		look around 环顾
give 短语	give up 放弃	put 短语	put up 搭建、张贴
	give in 屈服、让步		put on 穿上、上演
	give away 捐赠		put off 推迟
	give out 分发、散发		put out 熄灭、扑灭
	give off 发出（光、热等）		put away 把……收起来
（be）used to	be used to doing 习惯做某事		put down 写下、记下
	used to do sth. 过去常常做……事		put up with 容忍
	be used to do sth. 被用来做……		put...into 表达、翻译

专项练习题

一、用所给单词的适当形式填空

1. After following the doctor's advice, Michael looks _____（health）than before.

2. He always kept _____（silence）at meeting.

3. What Mr. White said sounds _____（nice）.

4. The moment I closed my eyes, I fell _____（sleep）.

5. If you don't eat anything, you will feel _____（hunger）.

6. The children all looked _____（sad）at the broken model plane and felt quite（sad）.

7. Vitamin D helps bones grow _____ (strong) .

8. This math problem is _____ (easy) and I can do it _____ (easy) .

9. Because of hunting, elephant numbers fell _____ (quick) .

10. If you make the wheels round, they will turn more _____ (easy) .

二、单项选择题

1. You _____ read in light which is too bright or too dim.

    A. need not   B. must not

    C. will not   D. dare not

2. You'd better hurry. The food is _____ cold.

    A. going   B. getting

    C. growing   D. changing

3. Even in the worst weather, poverty _____ them to go out.

    A. made   B. drove

    C. had   D. caught

4. This idea sounds _____ .

    A. well   B. good

    C. nicely   D. pleasantly

5. My father _____ me to become a scientist.

    A. hopes   B. advises

    C. suggests   D. thinks

6. You should adapt yourself _____ new ways of looking at matters.

    A. for   B. to

    C. from   D. of

7. An idea suddenly _____ to me when I looked out of window.

    A. happened   B. entered

    C. occurred   D. emerged

8. He spoke so quickly that I did not _____ what he said.

    A. take   B. catch

    C. accept   D. get

9. Did the mountain _____ far below?

    A. lie   B. lay

    C. lain   D. laid

10. Alex _____ me he had seen the play already.

    A. said   B. replied

    C. told   D. answered

11. Be careful! Your trousers will _____ fire if you stand there.

    A. light   B. catch

    C. get   D. burn

12. It's a very popular play, and it would be wise to _____ seats well in advance.

    A. book   B. buy

    C. occupy   D. take

13. Excuse me, John, do you think I could _____ your phone?

    A. use   B. lend

    C. carry   D. borrow

14. Quite a lot of people watch TV only to _____ time.

    A. waste   B. spend

    C. past   D. kill

15. Can you give another hit without _____ the answer?

    A. giving away   B. giving off

    C. giving up   D. giving in

16. If you don't _____ smoking you will never get recovered.

    A. give off   B. give in

    C. give out   D. give up

17. We must _____ the matter carefully to find out the truth.

    A. look after   B. look for

    C. look into   D. look over

18. The teacher didn't correct his composition because he couldn't _____ his handwriting.

    A. make out   B. point out

    C. look out   D. work out

19. If you want to telephone me, you will have to _____ his number in the book.

    A. look at   B. look to

    C. look through   D. look up

20. Three policemen were needed to _____ the fight.

    A. break up   B. break out

    C. break off   D. break down

21. She moved out to live alone because she couldn't ____ her father's bad temper any longer.

        A. catch up with   B. come up with   C. keep up with   D. put up with

22. Lucy will ____ her shyness once she stands on the stage.

        A. get away   B. get off   C. get through   D. get over

23. The real trouble ____ their lack of confidence in their abilities.

        A. lies in   B. lives on   C. results in   D. leads to

24. Americans move frequently from place to place. Born in one city, they may school in a second, and enter business a third.

        A. join   B. attend   C. participate   D. obtain

25. Last year the advertising rate ____ by 20 percent.

        A. raised   B. arose   C. aroused   D. rose

第八节　情态动词

一、情态动词的定义和特征

情态动词本身有词义，但不能独立使用，要和另一动词一起构成谓语，表示说话人的某种情绪，没有人称和数的变化。

英语中的情态动词主要有 can, could, may, might, must, should, ought to, will, would, shall, dare, need 等。

二、情态动词的基本用法

（一）can, could, may, might

情态动词	否定形式	疑问式与回答	用法
can	can not/can't	Can…do…? –Yes,…can –No,…can't.	1. 表示能力（体力、智力、技能） 2. 表示允许或请求（多用于口语） 3. 表示客观可能性 4. 表示猜测（惊讶、怀疑、不相信的态度），用于否定句或疑问句
could	could not/couldn't		

情态动词	否定形式	疑问式与回答	用法
may	may not	May…do…? –Yes,…may. –No,…mustn't/can't.	1. 可以（问句中表示请求，might 比 may 更委婉） 2. 表示推测，可能性（不用于疑问句中） 3. 表示祝愿（用于祈使句中）
might	might not	Might…do…? –Yes,…might. –No,…might not.	

Can you speak English?

When I was young, I could climb any tree in the forest.

Could you please speak a little louder?

Could this be true?

May I use your phone?

You may come if you wish.

May our friendship live long!

> ➤ can/could 与 is/am/are able to 的区别

（1）can 可与 is/am/are able to 互换使用，但在将来时和完成时中必须用 will be able to 和 have/has been able to。

Can you type? (=Are you able to type?)

We haven't been able to reach an agreement.

（2）表示经过努力成功地完成某一具体动作时，只能用 was/were able to, succeeded in 或 manage to，不能用 could；但如果表示某一动作没有成功，则可以使用 couldn't。

After years of hard work he was able to win the prize.

I couldn't/wasn't able to find the person I was looking for.

（二）must, should, ought to

情态动词	否定形式	疑问式与回答	用法	例句
must	must not/ mustn't	Must…do…? –Yes,…must –No,…needn't/ don't have to.	1. 必须、应该（表示主观要求） 2. 肯定、想必（肯定句中表示推测）	He must do as he is told. You mustn't smoke in the room.

情态动词	否定形式	疑问式与回答	用法	例句
should/ ought to	should not/ shouldn't ought not to/ oughtn't to	Ought…to do…? –Yes,…ought. –No,…oughtn't. Should…do…?	1. 应该、应当（表示义务责任 ought to 比 should 语气重） 2. 表示劝告、建议 3. should 用于疑问句或感叹句，表示意外、惊异等，与 how，why，who 连用。 4. should 用于从句中，表示虚拟的语气	I think today's children should/ought to really learn to respect their elders. Why should you be worrying? I suggest we should discuss it at once.
need	need not/ needn't	Need…do…? –Yes,…must. –No,…needn't.	需要、必须（常用于否定句和疑问句，在肯定句中一般用 must, have to, should, ought to）	You needn't have told her the news.

【注意 1】"should/ ought to have+ 过去分词"表示过去应该做某事而却没做；"shouldn't/ oughtn't to have+ 过去分词"表示过去本不该做某事却做了。"needn't +have+ 过去分词"表示过去没有必要做某事而却做了。

You should /ought to have told me about it.

You shouldn't/oughtn't to have lied to me.

You needn't have got up early.

【注意 2】need 作情态动词时，没有人称和数的变化，后接动词原形。作实义动词时，有人称和数的变化，后接动词不定式。当 need 后面接动名词时，表示被动含义。need doing = need to be done，意为"某物需要被……"。

You needn't talk so loud.

We didn't need to come.

The windows need cleaning.

=The windows need to be cleaned.

> ➤ must 与 have to 的区别
>
> must 强调主观看法，表示说话人主观上认为有必要做某事；have to 强调客观需要，有时态和人称的变化，表示因客观条件要求不得不做某事。
>
> She must do it herself. I shan't help her.
>
> She has to do it herself. She has got no one to help her.

（三）will/would（表示意愿和请求）

1. 表示请求，两者可互换使用，would 的语气更委婉，也可以用 won't

（1）提出邀请。

Will /Would/Won't you have a walk with me?

(Yes,) I'd like/love to. /No, I'd prefer not to, thank you.

（2）提出请求。

Will/Would you (please) open the door?

Yes, of course. /No, I'm afraid I can't.

2. 表示意图，意愿

He wouldn't come—he said he was too busy.

If you will try again, you will succeed.

3. 表示习惯或自然的倾向

（1）will 代替一般现在时，would 代替一般过去时，表示特有的习惯和行为。

In fine weather, he will often sit in the sun for hours.

She would spend hours in the bathroom or on the phone.

（2）当主语为第三人称时，will 表示真理或事物的品质。

Oil will float on water.

Fish will die out of water.

> ➤ would 与 used to 的区别
>
> （1）used to 强调如今已不存在的过去习惯性动作或状态，与现在的情况形成对比。
>
> He used to smoke a lot, (but he doesn't any longer).
>
> There used to be a church, (but now there isn't).
>
> （2）would 强调过去某种特定情况下的动作，是完全过去的事情，与现在没有关系。would 只表示动作，不表示状态。
>
> Sometimes she would take a walk in the park.
>
> Whenever I had difficulties, I would ask him for help.
>
> （3）used to 表示习惯性动作时，可以和 would 互换使用。
>
> When we were children, we used to/would swim every summer.
>
> She used to/would spend every penny she earned on clothes.

（四）shall（表示允许）

用于第一人称疑问句中，表示愿意按对方的指示去做。

1. 向对方提出建议

— Shall we meet in the evening?

— Yes, let's, (shall we)? /No, I'd rather not.

2. 提议为他人做事

— Shall I go there tomorrow?

— Yes, please. /No, thank you.

（五）dare（意为"敢于"）

1. 作情态动词时，没有人称和数的变化，后接动词原形，否定形式为 dare not 或 daren't，仅用于疑问句、条件句和否定句中

Dare you do it again?

If you dare call me that name again, you will be sorry.

She dare not go out at night.

2. 作实义动词时，有人称和数的变化，后接动词不定式

How did he dare to tell her?

We all knew that she was wrong, but none of us dared (to) tell her.

三、情态动词表示推测

情态动词表示推测，其肯定程度由低到高为 might → may → could → can → must

对现在或将来的情况表示推测，用"情态动词 +do"的形式；对现在或将来正在进行的情况表示推测，用"情态动词 +be doing"的形式；对已经发生的情况表示推测，用"情态动词 +have done"的形式。

情态动词	用法	例句
can	表示推测往往用于否定句和疑问句	That can't be Mary — She's in hospital. There's someone outside — Who can it be?
could	既可以表示过去的可能性，也可以表示现在的可能性，比 can 的可能性要弱	He said the news could be true. Someone is knocking at the door. Who could it be? You could be right, I suppose.
may/might	表示推测多用于肯定句。may 表示现在、将来的可能性；might 既可以表示过去的可能性，也可以表示现在、将来的可能性，比 may 的可能性要弱	He may/might come tomorrow, but I am not quite sure. She may/might be waiting for you now. He might have seen the film yesterday.
must	表示推荐意为"一定是""准是"，常指有根据的、比较有把握的推测，只用于肯定句中	Jack and Dick must be twins. They look so much alike.

专项练习题

1. You _____ return the book now. You can keep it till next week if you like.

    A. can't   B. mustn't

    C. needn't   D. may not

2. The work is too hard for him. He _____ finish it on time.

    A. can't   B. mustn't

    C. shouldn't   D. needn't

3. This dictionary _____ Tom's. It has Ann's name on it.

    A. might be   B. may be

    C. can't be   D. can be

4. ——May I go out now, Dad?

    ——No. You _____ let your mother know first.

    A. can   B. may

    C. need   D. must

5. You look quite tired. You'd better _____ a good rest.

    A. stop to have   B. stop doing

    C. to stop to have   D. to stop having

6. ——Must I water the flowers now. Mum?

    ——No, you _____ . You _____ do it later.

    A. mustn't, must   B. mustn't, may

    C. needn't, may   D. needn't, must

7. It rained heavily, so we _____ stay at home watching TV or surfing the Internet all day.

    A. could   B. had to

    C. must   D. may

8. Drunk driving is against the law now. It _____ be forbidden.

    A. may   B. must

    C. can   D. might

9. You _____ finish the report today. Any time before Friday is OK.

    A. mustn't   B. must

    C. need   D. needn't

10. The talented boy _____ write poems when he was at the age of six.

    A. may   B. could

    C. must   D. need

11. You _____ lose your way if you walk alone in the mountains at night.

    A. may   B. need

    C. should   D. ought to

12. It is usually warm in my hometown in March, but it _____ be rather cold sometimes.

    A. must   B. can

    C. should   D. would

13. We _____ the letter yesterday, but it didn't arrive.

    A, must receive   B. must have received

    C. ought to receive   D. ought to have received

14. If you _____ me, I shall be very grateful to you.

    A. helped   B. will help

    C. are helping   D. will be helping

15. You should not _____ him the news that day.

    A. tell   B. have told

    C. be telling   D. be told

16. I should have come to the movie, but I _____ too busy.

    A. was   B. were

    C. had been   D. am

17. When I was a student, I _____ take a walk along the country road on Sunday afternoons.

    A. might   B. could

    C. would   D. should

18. The English of the composition is too good. He _____ it himself.

    A. can't have written   B. mustn't have written

    C. won't have written   D. shouldn't have written

19. You _____ pay the money, but you _____ do so at once.

    A. needn't , must   B. need, need

    C. must, must   D. must, needn't

20. Tom, _____ you tell me what's the assignment for today?

    A. may   B. must

    C. could   D. might

21. ——Must I go through the security check when I am at the airport?

    ——Yes, you _____.

    A. can   B. may

C. might   D. must

22. Boys and girls, don't forget your report. It _____ today.

A. can't finish   B. can't be finished

C. should finish   D. should be finished

23. The swimmer was very tired but he _____ reach the shore.

A. might   B. could

C. was able to   D. succeeded to

24. She doesn't answer the doorbell. She _____ be asleep.

A. ought to   B. might

C. can   D. must have been

25. The line is busy, someone _____ the telephone now.

A. must use   B. must have used

C. must be using   D, must have been using

26. ——What is your mother going to do this Saturday?

——I'm not sure. She _____ go to see my grandmother.

A. can   B. must

C. may   D. should

27. He went on foot, but he _____ by bus.

A. should go   B. can go

C. would go   D. could have gone

28. You're right, I _____ of that.

A. should think   B. should have thought

C. must have thought   D. needn't think

29. He spent the weekend in the country as he_____ go to the office on Sunday.

A. mustn't   B. shouldn't

C. didn't have to   D. didn't need

30. No one _____ that to his face.

A. dares say   B. dares saying

C. dare say   D. dare to say

第九节 动词的时态

一、时态的种类

英语中共有十六种时态，常用的有十二种。

	一般	进行	完成	完成进行
现在	一般现在时	现在进行时	现在完成时	现在完成进行时
过去	一般过去时	过去进行时	过去完成时	过去完成进行时
将来	一般将来时	将来进行时	将来完成时	将来完成进行时
过去将来	过去将来时	过去将来进行时	过去将来完成时	过去将来完成进行时

二、一般现在时

（一）结构：主语 +am/is/are+ 表语

主语 + 动词原形（动词单数第三人称形式）+ 其他

（二）动词单数第三人称形式的变化规则

动词原形	规则	例词	
一般情况	加 s	run–runs say–says	write–writes play–plays
以字母 ch, sh, s, x 或 o 结尾	加 es	catch–catches wash–washes fix–fixes	teach–teaches guess–guesses go–goes
以"辅音字母 +y"结尾	变 y 为 i 再加 es	fly–flies try–tries	carry–carries worry–worries
have	has		

（三）意义

1. 表示表示习惯性或经常性存在的状态或动作

常与表示频率的时间状语连用，如 always, often, usually, generally, sometimes, rarely, never, once a week, twice a month, every day, now and then, on Sundays/Mondays.

Little children always fight among themselves.

They go to the movies once a week to relax themselves.

I talk with my parents by phone now and then.

2. 表示格言、客观事实或普遍真理

The sun rises in the east and sets in the west.

As we all know, the earth travels around the sun.

3. 表示事先安排好的动作或按时间表将要发生的动作或事件

常见的动词有 go, come, arrive, leave, stay, return, retire, take off, begin, start, stop, open 等。

The new project starts on the first day of May.

The plane takes off at 11 a.m.

4. 在时间或条件状语从句中，用一般现在时代替一般将来时

We will discuss the matter when we meet tomorrow.

I will not go to the countryside if it rains tomorrow.

三、一般过去时

（一）结构：主语 +was/were +adj./n./pron./ 介词短语（表示过去某时的状态）

主语 + 动词过去式 + 其他（发生于过去的动作）

（二）意义

表示过去某时间存在的状态或发生的动作。常与 yesterday, yesterday morning/afternoon/ evening, last year/week/night, three days ago, just now, in the past, in+ 过去的年份等连用。

The little girl didn't go on holiday with her parents last month.

He visited the Great Wall last year.

I'm calling you to ask about the apartment you advertised the other day.

（三）There be 句型的一般过去时

➤ There was+ 单数 n./ 不可数 n.+ 地点状语 + 时间

➤ There were+ 复数 n.+ 地点 + 时间

There was a book on the table yesterday.

There were books on the table yesterday.

（四）规则变化的动词过去式

动词原形	规则	例词
一般情况	加 –ed	worked, played, watched
以字母 e 结尾	直接加 –d	lived, moved
以"辅音字母 +y"结尾	变 y 为 i 再加 –ed	carried, tried, worried

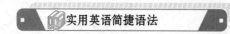

续表

动词原形	规则	例词
以重读闭音节结尾，末尾只有一个辅音字母	双写末尾字母再加 –ed	planned, preferred, occurred

※ 不规则变化的动词过去式详见本节附录。

四、一般将来时

（一）结构：主语 +will/shall+ 动词原形

主语 +am/is/are going to+ 动词原形

主语 +am/is/are to+ 动词原形

主语 +am/is/are about+ 不定式

主语 +am/is/are+ 现在分词

（二）标志词

1. tomorrow 明天

tomorrow morning/afternoon/evening/night

the day after tomorrow

2. next week 下周

next Sunday/Monday/year/month

3. in+ 将来的年份

In 2030

4. soon 不久

5. in+ 一段时间

in two days 两天以后 = in two days' time

in a day 一天以后 = in a day's time

in ten years 十年以后 = in ten years' time

He is going to paint the house in two days.

How soon is he going to paint the house?

6. in the future 将来

from now on 从今以后

（三）意义

1. "will/shall + 动词原形"表示将要发生的动作或状态。shall 常用于第一人称，will 可用于各个人称

My elder brother will be thirty years old next year.

2. "am/is/are going to+ 动词原形" 表示主管打算做某事或有迹象标明即将发生某事

They are going to sail around the small island.

It is cloudy. I think it is going to rain soon.

3. "am/is/are to+ 动词原形" 表示按安排、计划、约定、职责、义务或要求必须做的事或即将发生的动作

Your assignment is to be handed in next Tuesday.

You are not to tell her anything about our plan.

4. "am/is/are about + 不定式" 表示即将发生的动作，不能与表示将来的时间状语连用

We are about to leave, so there is no time to drop in on her now.

The team is about to play an important match.

5. "am/is/are + 现在分词" 可表示在不久的将来要做某事，或按计划、安排将要发生某事

常见这类动词有：go, come, leave, start, begin, arrive, stay, take 等。

She is leaving for Shanghai in three days.

6. 在 "祈使句 + and/or + 陈述句" 结构中，前面的祈使句表示条件，and/or 后面的句子用将来时

Give me one more hour, and I'll get the work finished.

Close the window, or you'll catch a cold.

7. There be 句型的将来时结构，表示 "某地将要有某物 / 某人"。

（1）There be（is/am/are）going to be+ 主语 + 地点 + 时间。

There is going to be a tiger in the zoo next year.

明年动物园里将会有一只老虎。

There are going to be two football games on CCTV-5 tonight.

今天晚上中央五台将会有两场足球赛。

（2）There will be+ 主语 + 地点 + 时间。

There will be an NBA basketball game in ten minutes.

---

be going to do 与 will/shall do

※be going to	※will/shall do
1. 含有打算、计划、准备等含义	1. 表示较远的时间里将要发生的事情
2. 通常表示近期就要发生的事情	2. 客观上将要发生的事实
3. 根据迹象标明马上就要发生的事情	It will be Tuesday tomorrow.

He is going to write a letter tonight.

Look at these clouds. It is going to rain.

五、现在进行时

（一）结构：主语 + is/am/are + 动词的现在分词

（二）动词现在分词的变化规则

动词原形	规则	例词
一般情况	加 –ing	working, playing, watching
以字母 e 结尾	去 e 加 –ing（e 不发音）	living, moving, making
	直接加 –ing	seeing, dyeing, ageing, toeing
	变 ie 为 y，加 –ing	die–dying, lie–lying, tie–tying
以重读闭音节结尾，末尾只有一个辅音字母	双写末尾字母再加 –ing	planning, beginning, sitting
以字母 c 结尾	加 k 再加 –ing	picnicking, panicking

（三）意义

1. 表示现在、目前或现阶段正在进行的动作或发生的事情

常与 now, at the moment, Look! Listen! 等标志词连用。

We are waiting for you at the school gate now.

Today the number of people learning English in China is increasing rapidly.

2. 与 always, forever, constantly 等副词连用，表示某种感情，如赞许、厌烦、不满、同情等

The little boy is always thinking of others.

He is always making trouble for his friends.

（四）下列动词（短语）不能用于进行时态

（1）表示感情状态，如 love, adore, prefer, like, hate, detest 等。

（2）表示感知、感觉、知觉，如 see, hear, taste, smell, appear, look, sound 等。

（3）表示理解、思考等心理活动，如 realize, know, remember, believe, forget, understand 等。

（4）表示存在的状态，如 exist, stay, remain, obtain 等。

（5）表示所属关系，如 have, contain, belong to, own, possess, consist of 等。

六、过去进行时

（一）结构：主语 +was/were+ 现在分词

（二）意义

1. 表示过去某个时间点正在发生的动作，或过去某段时间内持续做的事情

常与 at 7 o'clock yesterday, at that time/then, at this time yesterday, from 7 to 8 yesterday, the whole morning/all morning 等时间状语连用。

My mother was cooking at 7 o'clock yesterday morning.

I was watching TV at that time.

Bob was doing homework from 7 o'clock to 8 o'clock last night.

2. 过去某个正在发生的动作突然被另一个动作打断

（1）when 引导的时间状语从句，当……时候，就在这个时候（从句过去进行时，主句一般过去时）。

When I was reading books, my mother came in.

When we were playing on the playground, it began to rain.

When I was walking on the road, I met Peter.

I was watching TV, when my mother came back.

I was cooking in the kitchen when the telephone rang.

（2）while 引导的时间状语从句，当……时候。

① while 所在从句的谓语动词为延续性动词，从句时态用过去进行时；主句为瞬间性动词，主句时态用一般过去时。

While Mary was typing a letter, the boss came in.

② while 引导的句子，若从句和主句的谓语动词都是延续性动词，时态都用过去进行时。

While my mother was cooking in the kitchen, my father was watching TV.

七、将来进行时

（一）结构："主语 +shall/will+ be+ 动词现在分词"

【注意】shall 仅限于第一人称，will 可用于所有人称。

（二）意义

表示在将来某一时刻或某段时间内正在进行的动作，或按计划在将来某一时刻或某短时间内将要进行的动作。

We shall be working in that factory this time tomorrow.

I won't be free Friday morning. — I'll be seeing a friend off.

She's singing an English song, and later she will be dancing.

八、现在完成时

（一）结构：主语 + have/has + 动词的过去分词（动词过去分词的规则变化同动词过去式，不规则变化详见本节附录）

（二）意义

1. 表示动作发生于过去，对现在产生一定影响。常与以下时间状语连用

（1）already "已经"，常放在 have / has 后面，多用于肯定句，用在疑问句中表示特殊的语气。

I have already finished my homework.

He has already had lunch.

（2）yet 还、已经，放在句末，用于疑问句和否定句中。

Have you finished your homework yet?

He hasn't had lunch yet.

（3）just 刚刚，放在 have/has 后面。

I have just watched TV.

【注意】just now（刚才）用于过去时。

I watched TV just now.

（4）ever 曾经，放在 have/has 后面，常用于肯定句和疑问句中。

I have ever seen that film.

Have you ever seen that film?

（5）before 以前、之前，放在句末。

Have you read this book before?

（6）never 从未，用于陈述句，所在的句子为否定句。

I have never seen him.

【注意】区分 never 在以下两个句子中的不同时态。

I have never drunk beer.（我从未喝过啤酒）

I never drinks beer.（我从不喝啤酒）

（7）so far 至今、到目前为止，可放于句首或句末。

We have learnt two thousand words so far.

现在完成时态中的"去过"和"去了"

※ 去过某地（说明人已返回）

have/has been to+ 地点名词　　My father has been to Japanese three times.

have/has been+ 地点副词 My father has been there three times.

※ 去了某地（说明人未回）

have/has gone to+ 地点名词　　Peter has gone to Beijing and he's coming back tomorrow.

have/has gone+ 地点副词 The boss has gone there.

2. 动作发生于过去，一直持续到现在，未来有可能还会持续下去。

【注意】此意义下动词必须是延续性动词，例如：live, study, teach, eat, drink 等。

（1）主语 + have/has done + for + 一段时间。

I have worked here for eight months.

We have already learnt English for three years.

I have lived in Jinzhou for ten years.

（2）主语 + have/has done +since+ 过去的某个时间。

I have worked here since three years ago.

= I have worked here for three years.

【注意】就 for/since + 时间提问，特殊疑问词用 how long。

We have learnt English since three years ago.

How long have you learnt English?

（3）It is/has been + 时间 + since + 表示一般过去式的句子。

It is /has been ten years since I bought this house.

It is/has been fifteen years since I worked here.

关于 since

※ 作介词（自从……）

since + 具体的表示过去的时间

since yesterday/last year/three years ago/ 1997/then/January/Sunday/7 o'clock

Tom lived in the town since ten years ago.

※ 作连词（从属连词，连接时间状语从句）

since+ 表示一般过去时的句子

自从我住在这儿 since I lived here

自从我遇到鲍勃 since I met Bob

（三）瞬间性意义转延续性意义

1. 瞬间性动词

动作从开始到结束持续的时间很短，瞬间开始又瞬间结束，不与一段时间连用。

He has already left.（他已经离开了。）

He left three days ago.（他三天前离开了。）

他离开已经三天了。

He has already left for three days.（ × ）

He has been away for three days.（ √ ）

【注意】be away 表示"离开"的状态。

He has already died.（他已经去世了。）

He died ten years ago.（他 10 年前去世了。）

他已经去世 10 年了。

He has already died for ten years.（ × ）

He has been dead for ten years.（ √ ）

【注意】be dead 表示"去世"的状态。

2. 瞬间性动词转延续性动词 / 状态

（1）die（v）→ be dead。

He died three years ago.

He has been dead for three years（since three years ago）.

It is（has been）three years since he died.

（2）buy（v）→ have。

I bought this house ten years ago.

I have had this house for ten years（since ten years ago）.

It is（has been）ten years since I bought this house.

（3）open → be open。

The shop opened two days ago.

The shop has been open for two days（since two days ago）.

It is（has been）two hours since the shop opened.

（4）close → be closed。

The supermarket closed two hours ago.

The supermarket has been closed for two hours（since two hours ago）.

It is（has been）two hours since the supermarket closed.

（5）begin → be on。

The film began twenty minutes ago.

The film has been on for twenty minutes（since twenty minutes ago）.

It is（has been）twenty minutes since the film began.

（6）leave → be away。

He left three days ago.

He has been away for three days（since three days ago）.

It is（has been）three days since he left.

（7）leave sp. → be away from sp.。

He left Beijing ten months ago.

He has been away from Beijing for ten months（since ten months ago）.

It is（has been）ten months since he left Beijing.

（8）arrive in → be in。

arrive at → be at

arrive at school → be at school

arrive home → be at home

arrive here/there → be here/there

I arrived in Shanghai an hour ago.

I have been in Shanghai for an hour（since an hour ago）.

It is（has been）an hour since I arrived in Shanghai.

（9）go/come/move to sp. → be in sp.。

He has gone to London.

He has been in London for three days.

九、过去完成时

（一）结构：主语 +had+ 动词过去分词

（二）意义

（1）表示在过去某个时间或某个动作之前已经完成的动作，或者表示从过去某个时间开始一直延续到过去另一个时间的动作。它表示动作发生的时间是"过去的过去"。常与含有 by, before, by the end of 等介词（短语）的时间状语或宾语 by the time，before 等引导的时间状语从句连用，也可以通过上下文含义来表示。

I had just finished half of the work before my parents come back.

By the time they finished the job, we had reached home.

She found that she had left her luggage on the bus.

（2）过去完成时常用在 hardly/scarcely…when 和 no sooner…than 结构的主句中。

She had hardly/scarcely gone to bed when the bell rang.

We had no sooner entered the room than it began to rain.

No sooner had he opened his mouth than I knew what he wanted to say.

（3）intend, mean, hope, want, expect, think 等动词的过去完成时形式，表示"本打算做某事而未做"。

I had wanted to invite her to the party.

We had meant to tell her the news but found she wasn't in.

（4）在包含由 after, before 引导的时间状语从句中，如果两个动作紧接着发生，常常用一般过去时代替过去完成时。

The train had left（=left）before I reached the station.

We ate our lunch after my wife had come back（=came back）from her shopping.

十、将来完成时

（一）结构：主语 +shall/will have+ 动词过去分词

（二）意义

1. 表示将来某时之前或某动作发生之前已经完成的动作

They will have graduated from the university before next year.

I shall/will have moved into the new house by the end of this week.

2. 表示一个持续到将来某时或某个动作发生时的动作

By next Sunday he will have lived in London for twenty years.

The concert will begin at 9 p.m. They will have played half an hour when we arrive.

十一、过去将来时

（一）结构：主语 +should/would+ 动词原形

（二）意义

1. 表示从过去某时看将来发生的动作或状态

He said that he would come and see me the next week.

She hoped that they would meet again someday.

2. 表示过去将来的其他用法

（1）was/were going to 表示过去的打算，也可以表示未实现的动作。

He was going to leave when you arrived.

He was going to come last night, but it rained.

（2）was/were to 表示曾计划做的事。表示计划的动作未实现，要用"was/were to

have+ 过去分词"形式。

He said that they were to leave at 6.

I was to have seen him last Wednesday, but he didn't come.

（3）was/were about to 表示过去即将发生的动作，不能用表示时间的副词作状语，但可以带由 when, as 等引导的时间状语从句。

When I saw Tom, he was just about to get on the bus.

We were about to start when it rained.

十二、现在完成进行时

（一）结构：主语 +have/has been + 现在分词

（二）意义

（1）表示在过去某时开始发生，一直延续到现在并继续延续下去的动作，可以和表示一段的时间状语 for two hours, since early morning, all these years 等连用。

I've been waiting for an hour but she still hasn't come.

It has been raining since last Sunday.

The children have been watching TV all evening.

（2）表示在过去某时开始发生，一直延续到现在，在说话时已经结束的动作。

The road is slippery. It has been raining.

I'm very tired. I've been playing football.

十三、过去完成进行时

（一）结构：主语 +have/has been + 现在分词

（二）意义：表示过去某个时间之前一直在进行的动作或状态

I didn't know he had been suffering from such great pain.

I had been studying English before I went to college.

专项练习题

一、写出下列句子的时态

1. He came to see me this morning.

2. He has been abroad for six months.

3. The teacher often tells me stories.

4. He is ill, and he is lying in bed now.

5. Have you ever met him before?

6. Workers are cleaning the street now.

7. There were students everywhere.

8. They haven't found the parcel yet.

9. Are you and Tom in the same class?

10. After coming in, they took off the shoes.

11. I've waited for you for half an hour.

12. He felt cold, so he put on his coat.

二、用动词的适当形式填空

1. She _____ on her coat and went out. (put)

2. "What are they doing?" "They _____ ready for the sports meeting." (get)

3. It _____ (take) him half an hour _____ (finish) his homework yesterday.

4. They usually _____ (do) their homework after supper.

5. Listen! Who _____ (sing) in the next room now?

6. _____ (be) your parents in Shanghai last year?

7. Mr. Yu _____ (teach) us maths since 1982.

8. Yesterday she _____ (want) to see the film, but she couldn't _____ (get) a ticket.

9. Mike _____ (visit) several places since he came to Beijing.

10. He _____ (write) four letters to his wife every month.

11. There _____ (be) a meeting next Monday.

12. We _____ (know) each other since our boyhood.

13. Sometimes my father _____ (come) back home late.

14. They _____ (have) an English contest next week.

15. Wei Fang ins't here. She _____ (go) to the reading–room.

16. The story _____ (happen) long ago.

17. Look! The young worker _____ (show) the students around the factory now.

18. The boys _____ (have) a basketball match now. Let's _____ (go) and _____ (watch) .

19. How long_____the Smiths _____ (stay) here ? For two weeks.

20. _____ you _____ (find) your science book yet?

三、用 "never, ever, already, just, yet, for, since" 填空

1. I have ＿＿ seen him before, so I have no idea about him.

2. Jack has ＿＿ finished his homework.

3. Mr. Wang has taught in this school ＿＿ ten years.

4. "Have you ＿＿ seen the film?" "No, I have ＿＿ seen it."

5. "Has the bus left ＿＿ ?" "Yes, it has ＿＿ left."

四、单项选择

1. Since he came here last year, we ＿＿ happy.
   A. are   B. have been
   C. had been   D. were

2. Peter ＿＿ the work in a week.
   A .have finished   B. finishes
   C.is finishing   D. will finish

3. ＿＿ open the window.
   A. Will you please   B. Please will you
   C. You please   D. Please

4. Many sheep ＿＿ eating grass.
   A.is   B. are
   C. was   D.be

5. The Green family ＿＿ London for nearly two years. They all miss their hometown very much.
   A. left   B. will leave
   C. have left   D. have been away from

6. Her grandparents ＿＿ for ten years.
   A. died   B. have died
   C. were dead   D. have been dead

7. When ＿＿ you ＿＿ the museum?
   A. would, visit   B. did, visit
   C. have, visit   D. had, visited

8. The sick man stayed in bed and ＿＿ very terrible.
   A. felt   B. feeling
   C. is feeling   D. was feeling

9. —How was your weekend on the farm?

　— Great! We ＿＿ with the farmers.

　　A. enjoy ourselves　　　　B. went fishing

　　C. will work　　　　　　　D. make friends

10. —What did Mr. Jones do before he moved here?

　　— He ＿＿ a city bus for over twenty–five years.

　　A.is driving　　　　　　　B. drove

　　C. has driven　　　　　　　D. drives

11. He turned off the light and then ＿＿.

　　A. leaves　　　　　　　　　B. has left

　　C. will leave　　　　　　　D. left

12. Father usually ＿＿ his newspaper after dinner.

　　A. read　　　　　　　　　　B. reads

　　C. reading　　　　　　　　D. is reading

13. The Blacks often ＿＿ to the cinema on Saturday evenings.

　　A. go　　　　　　　　　　　B. goes

　　C. is going　　　　　　　　D. are going

14. Look! The boy ＿＿ with his mother in the pool.

　　A. is swimming　　　　　　B. is swimming

　　C. are swimming　　　　　D. are swimming

15. —What is Tom doing in the classroom?

　　—He ＿＿ something on the blackboard.

　　A. draws　　　　　　　　　B. draw

　　C. is drawing　　　　　　　D. are drawing

16. Old Tom usually ＿＿ up at six and ＿＿ sports in the garden.

　　A. gets, dos　　　　　　　B. gets, does

　　C. get, does　　　　　　　D. gets, do

17. It's ten o'clock and Jack ＿＿ still ＿＿ his homework.

　　A. is, do　　　　　　　　　B. is, doing

　　C. are, do　　　　　　　　D. are, doing

18. The waiters ＿＿ to work at five every morning.

　　A. start　　　　　　　　　B. starts

　　C. starting　　　　　　　　D. are starting

19. I ＿＿＿ a letter, so I can't go out with you.

    A. is writing　　　　　　　B. am writing

    C. am writeing　　　　　　D. am writting

20. —＿＿＿ late for the meeting next time.

    —Sorry, I won't.

    A. Don't　　　　　　　　B. Don't be

    C. Won't be　　　　　　　D. Be not

21. My mother ＿＿＿ noodles, but my father ＿＿＿.

    A. likes, doesn't　　　　　B. don't like, do

    C. likes, didn't　　　　　　D. didn't like, do

22. —Does she have a watch?

    —Yes, she ＿＿＿.

    A. have　　　　　　　　B. do

    C. has　　　　　　　　　D. does

23. She ＿＿＿ English very much now.

    A. is liking　　　　　　　B. likes

    C. liked　　　　　　　　D. is teaching

24. Does your mother ＿＿＿ English now?

    A. teaches　　　　　　　B. teach

    C. taught　　　　　　　　D. is teaching

25. Jack usually ＿＿＿ mistakes last term. But this term he does better.

    A. makes　　　　　　　　B. made

    C. does　　　　　　　　　D. did

26. The boy is too young, please ＿＿＿ carefully.

    A. look after him　　　　　B. look him after

    C. look at him　　　　　　D. look him at

27. Bob often ＿＿＿ his mother with the housework on Sundays.

    A. help　　　　　　　　B. helping

    C. helps　　　　　　　　D. helped

28.The supermarket is far from Mary's house. So she ＿＿＿ only once a week.

    A. goes shopping　　　　B. has been there

    C. was shopping　　　　　D. has gone there

29. Don't make so much noise. We ＿＿＿ to the music.

    A. are listening　　　　　B. listen

C. listened   D. have listened

30. There _____ a talk on science in our school next Monday.

    A. will give   B. will be

    C. is   D. is going to give

31. — Shall we go shopping now?

    — Sorry, I can't. I _____ my shirts.

    A. wash   B. washes

    C. washed   D. am washing

32. How long have you _____ here?

    A. come   B. got

    C. arrived   D. been

33. —What a nice dress! How long _____ you_____ it?

    —Just 2 weeks.

    A. will, buy   B. did, buy

    C. are, having   D. have, had

34. —Do you know Lydia very well?

    —Yes, She and I _____ friends since we were very young.

    A. have made   B. have become

    C. have been   D. have turned

35. The Smiths _____ in China for 8 years.

    A. has lived   B. lived

    C. have been   D. live

36. —Hello, this is Mr. Green speaking. Can I speak to Mr. Black?

    —Sorry. He _____ the Bainiao Park.

    A. has been to   B. has gone to

    C. went to   D. will go to

37. —_____ you ever _____ to the US?

    — Yes, twice.

    A. Have, gone   B. Have, been

    C, Do, go   D. were, going

38. —Why is Grace's Chinese so good?

    —Because she _____ China for ten years.

    A. has gone to   B. has been to

    C. has come to   D. has been in

39. Peter won't be surprised because I ____ him the news already.

    A. told   B. will tell

    C. have told   D. telling

40. I like this watch very much. I ____ it for five years.

    A. have had   B. had

    C. have bought   D. bought

41. Our school life ____ a lot since 2018. We have more activities now.

    A. change   B. changed

    C. will change   D. has changed

42. My father ____ in a panda protection center for ten years, so he knows a lot about pandas.

    A. was working   B. is working

    C. has worked   D. will work

43. By the end of April, I ____ here for three months.

    A. will stay   B. stays

    C. has stayed   D. will have stayed

44. The manager wants to know if they ____ our letter yet.

    A. will answer   B. answered

    C. have answered   D. had answered

45. A long time ago, Irving ____ in London.

    A. had lived   B. has lived

    C. lived   D. has been living

46. I had scarcely locked the door when the key____.

    A. breaks   B. was breaking

    C. had broken   D. broke

47. There ____ little change in the patient's condition since he was taken to the hospital.

    A. is   B. has been

    C. have been   D. was

48. Turn on the TV and you ____ advertisements showing happy families.

    A. are often seeing   B. will often see

    C. often see   D. have often seen

49. No sooner _____ one task than she was asked to do another.

    A. she had finished   B. had she finished

    C. he finished   D. could he finish

50. She said that she _____ the position, but later changed her mind.

    A. was to take up   B. was to have taken up

    C. would be taking   D. would take

附录：常见不规则变化动词的过去式和过去分词

A–A–A 型		
beat–beat–beat hit–hit–hit put–put–put	cost–cost –cost hurt–hurt–hurt read–read–read	cut–cut–cut let–let–let set –set–set
A–B–B 型		
babysit–babysat–babysat build–built–built fell–felt–felt forget –forgot–forgot hear–heard–heard lay–laid–laid learn–learnt–learnt mean–meant–meant say–said–said sit–sat–sat spell–spelt–spelt teach–taught–taught win–won–won	bring–brought–brought catch–caught–caught fight–fought–fought get–got–got hold–held–held leave–left–left lose–lost–lost meet–met–met sell–sold–sold sleep–slept–slept stand–stood–stood tell–told–told understand–understood–understood	buy–bought–bought feed–fed–fed find–found–found hang–hung–hung keep–kept–kept lend–lent–lent make–made–made pay–paid–paid send–sent–sent spend–spent–spent sweep–swept–swept think–thought–thought did–dud–dug
A–B–A 型		
become–became–become	come–came–come	run–ran–run
A–B–C 型		
am/is–was–been begin–began–begun draw–drew–drawn eat–ate–eaten freeze–froze–frozen grow–grew–grown ring–rang–rung speak–spoke–spoken throw–threw–thrown	are–were–been break–broke–broken drink–drank–drunk fall–fell–fallen give–gave–given know–knew–known see–saw–seen swim–swam–swum wear–wore–worn	bear–bore–born do–did–done drive–drove–driven fly–flew–flown go–went–gone ride–rode–ridden sing–sang–sung take–took–taken write–wrote–written
AAB 型		
beat–beat–beaten		

第十节 动词的语态

一、定义

语态是表示主语和谓语之间关系的一种动词形式。英语有两种语态：主动语态和被动语态。主动语态表示主语是动作的执行者，被动语态表示主语是动作的承受者。

Peter is reading a book.

A book is being read by Peter.

二、被动语态的构成

被动语态中动词的基本结构为"be+ 过去分词"，动作的执行者由"by+ 名词或人称代词宾格"表示。助动词 be 有人称、数和时态的变化。英语被动语态的各种时态形式，以动词 do 为例，列表如下：

时态	被动语态	例句	
		主动语态	被动语态
一般现在时	is/am/are done	We clean the room.	The room is cleaned by us.
现在进行时	is/am/are being done	She is watering the flowers.	The flowers are being watered by her.
现在完成时	has/have been done	Jim has finished the work.	The work has been finished by Jim.
一般过去时	was/were done	He made the kite.	The kite was made by him.
过去进行时	was/were being done	She was writing a letter this time yesterday.	A letter was being written by her this time yesterday.
过去完成时	had been done	Jim had finished the work by last week.	The work had been finished by Jim by last week.
一般将来时	will/shall be done	They will plant trees tomorrow.	Trees will be planted by them tomorrow.
将来完成时	will/shall have been done	People will have opened this oil field by the end of next month.	This oil field will have been opened by the end of next month.
过去将来时	would/should be done	He said he would make a model plane.	He said a model plane would be made by him.
过去将来完成时	would/should have been	He said he would have finished his homework by ten o'clock.	He said his homework would have been finished by him by ten o'clock.
含情态动词	can/may/must…be done	I can find it.	It can be found by me.

三、被动语态的基本用法

1. 不知道或没有必要说出动作的执行者，不带由 by 构成的介词短语

The book was written in 1896.

Printing was introduced into Europe from China.

2. 强调动作的承受者，通常带由 by 构成的介词短语

The electric light was invented by Edison.

This mistake is committed by everyone.

3. 并非所有动词都有被动语态形式，不及物动词、系动词不能用于被动语态

常见这类动词有：appear, rise, die, happen, occur, lie, depart, belong to, break out, take place 等。表示状态的动词不能用于被动语态，常见的有：lack, fit, mean, hold, resemble, have, cost, contain, suit, become, last, possess, fail, consist of, look like 等。

This bookshelf belongs to me.

The war broke out in 1945.

The book costs 20 yuan.

The committee consists of ten members.

四、主动语态和被动语态的转换

1. 带双宾语的动词被动语态

给予动词 give, ask, allow, teach, tell, bring 等后面可以接双宾语，变成被动语态时，可将主动结构中的一个宾语变成被动语态中的主语，另一个宾语保持不变。如果把直接宾语变成主语，间接宾语前要加 to 或 for。

The boss gave him a chance. → He was given a chance. → A chance was given to him.

Her mother bought her a shirt. → She was bought a shirt. → A shirt was bought for her.

2. 使役动词 make, let, have 或感官动词 see, hear, watch, notice, feel, observe 等变成被动语态时，to 不可省略

She saw the thief enter the bank. → The thief was seen to enter the bank.

They made me repeat the story. → I was made to repeat the story.

3. 带宾语补足语的动词变被动语态时，主动句中的宾语变成被动句中的主语，宾语补足语相应变成了主语补足语

He painted the wall blue. → The wall was painted blue.

We found him surrounded by the enemy. → He were found surrounded by the enemy.

I heard Jane playing the piano in her room. → Jane was heard playing the piano in her room.

4. 动词短语的被动语态

（1）相当于及物动词的短语动词变成被动语态时，构成动词短语的介词、副词或其他词类不可省略。

People looked down upon him in the past. → He was looked down upon in the past.

They have sent for the doctor. → The doctor has been sent for.

（2）pay attention to, take care of, make use of, place emphasis on, attach importance to 等"动名介"型短语动词可以有两种形式的被动语态。

She took good care of the wounded.

→ The wounded was taken good care of.

→ Good care was taken of the wounded.

五、动词的主动形式表示被动含义

1. 感官动词或系动词，如：look, smell, taste, feel, prove, sound 等接形容词可以表示被动意义

The flower smells sweet.

The soup tasted delicious.

2. 某些及物动词，如：wash, write, sell, read, open, cut, lock, let, pack, shut, clean, eat 等加副词 well, easily 可以表示被动意义

The vegetable sells well.

The meat cuts easily.

3. 某些不及物动词与情态动词 can't, won't 连用表示被动意义

有些动词，如：move, lock, shut, open 等既可以作及物动词，也可以作不及物动词。作不及物动词时，虽然没有被动语态形式，但却可以和情态动词 can't, won't, wouldn't 等连用，表示被动的意义，意为"就是不……"。

The door won't shut.

The drawer wouldn't open.

专项练习题

一、用所给单词的适当形式填空

1. The leaves have ＿＿＿（turn）red.

2. The car ____ (make) in Shanghai in 2019.

3. Your homework should ____ (hand) in tomorrow.

4. That play ____ (put) on again sometime next month.

5. The windows are very dirty. They need ____ (clean) .

6. The book ____ (sell) well; it's a best-seller.

7. These famous stories ____ (write) a long time ago.

8. The Second World War ____ (break) out in 1939.

9. The sports meeting ____ (hold) next month.

10. They were watching TV when the power ____ (cut) off.

11. This pair of shoes ____ (fit) me well.

12. A new library ____ (build) in our school next year.

13. It ____ (report) that the President had suffered a heart attack.

14. The hot weather will ____ (last) until September.

15. Where did you have your hair ____ (cut) ?

二、单项选择题

1. Many accidents ____ by careless drivers last year.

    A. are caused   B. were caused

    C. have caused   D. will cause

2. An official ____ by some reporters on food problems in Shanghai yesterday.

    A. is interviewing   B. is interviewed

    C. was interviewing   D. was interviewed

3. Today a lot of information can ____ online.

    A. receive   B. be received

    C. is received   D. receiving

4. Driving after drinking wine ____ in China.

    A. allows   B. doesn't allow

    C. is allowed   D. ins't allowed

5. The Spring Festival ____ in January or February every year.

    A. celebrates   B. is celebrated

    C. celebrated   D. was celebrated

6. A friendly basketball match between teachers and students ____ tomorrow afternoon.

    A. was held   B. will be held

C. is held   D. was being held

7. It will be two days before the decision ____.

 A. has made   B. will be made

 C. was made   D. is made

8. At last the boy was made ____ and began to laugh.

 A. stop crying   B. to stop to cry

 C. to stop crying   D. stop to cry

9. The work ____ by the time you get there.

 A. is done   B. will have been done

 C. would have done   D. had been done

10. Train tickets ____ online. It is convenient.

 A. sold   B. were sold

 C. are sold   D. have sold

11. Food safety is important. Rules ____ to stop people from food pollution.

 A. must make   B. must be made

 C. can't make   D. can't be made

12. Mary didn't go to John's birthday party because she ____.

 A. wasn't invited   B. didn't invite

 C. ins't invited   D. invited

13. Boys and girls, the books in the library should ____ good care of.

 A. take   B. are taking

 C. be taken   D. be take

14. Half of the work ____ by now.

 A. has finished   B. has been finished

 C. have been finished   D. have finished

15. He likes reading very much. Most of his money ____ on books.

 A. is spent   B. spend

 C. spends   D. are spent

16. In the past, some children were made ____ 15 hours a day.

 A. to lock   B. work

 C. to work   D. lock

17. The news ____ to the public yet. Only a few people know.

 A. hasn't told   B. has been told

 C. hasn't been told   D. has told

18. Keep quiet, please! Talking _____ during the meeting.

    A. is not allowed   B. is allowed

    C. doesn't allow   D. allows

19. He is very surprised that all the houses in the village _____ white.

    A. paint   B. painted

    C. are painting   D. are painted

20. The task _____ in an hour. Then we can go home and have a good rest.

    A. was finished   B. will be finished

    C. has been finished   D. can't be finished

21. It's a custom in China to have some tea or other drinks before the meal _____.

    A. serves   B. served

    C. is served   D. will be served

22. In the past few years, thousands of films _____ all over the world.

    A. have produced   B. have been produced

    C. are producing   D. are being produced

23. These oranges _____ nice.

    A. are tasted   B. taste

    C. is tasted   D. tastes

24. The pen you sent me as a present _____.

    A. is written well   B. writes well

    C. is writing well   D. has well written

25. What kind of advice_____ you?

    A. has given to   B. was given for

    C. has been given to   D. has given

26. The children _____ many times not to go near the stove.

    A. have told   B. told

    C. have been told   D. were being told

27. An atom _____ three kinds of particles.

    A. makes up   B. is made of

    C. is consisted of   D. is composed of

28. On the way to work, it _____ to him that he had forgotten to turn off the gas in a hurry.

    A. occurred   B. was occurred

    C. had been occurred   D. had occurred

29. I ＿＿ at the same place more than 12 years now.

    A. employed   B. have been employed

    C. was being employed   D. have been employing

30. All the machines ＿＿ by the end of next week.

    A. would have been repaired   B. will have been repaired

    C. would repaired   D. were being repaired

第十一节　动词的语气

一、定义和分类

（一）定义：语气是动词形式，用来表示讲话人对某种言行或某件事的看法或态度

（二）分类：英语动词有三种语气：陈述语气，祈使语气和虚拟语气

动词的语气	功能作用	例句
陈述语气	用来叙述事实或可能发生的事情	I don't care what he thinks. Did you hear the news?
祈使语气	用来表示命令、要求、请求、邀请、劝告或建议等	Speak more slowly, please. Never shut that door!
虚拟语气	用来表示动作或状态不是客观存在的，而是想象、假设或愿望等	If I knew his number, I would tell you. I wish I had your brains.

二、虚拟语气的用法

（一）虚拟语气在状语从句中的用法

1. 用于 if 引导的非真实条件状语从句

（1）基本用法。

	从句动词的形式	主句动词的形式
表示与过去事实相反的情况	had + 过去分词	would/should/could/might + have +done
表示与现在事实相反或现在实际上并不存在的情况	动词过去式（were）	would/should/could/might + do
表示将来实现可能性不大的情况	should+ 动词原形 were to + 动词原形 动词过去式（were）	would/should/could/might + do

If I had left a little earlier, I would have caught the bus.

If I were you/in your position, I should not give up.

If you were to come next week, you would see him.

If it snowed tomorrow, I should stay at home.

（2）省略 if 的非真实条件句。

条件从句中有 were, had 或 should 时，可将 if 省略，将 were, had, should 放在主语之前，构成倒装。

Were she my daughter, I wouldn't allow her to marry a foreigner.

Had I known your address, I should have written to you.

Should anybody call, say I shall not be home till evening.

（3）错综虚拟条件句。

当从句和主句的动作发生的时间不一致时，从句和主句的动词按各自的时间变化。

If the doctor had come last night, Alice would be alive today.

If you didn't make up your mind now, you might suffer in future.

（4）含蓄虚拟条件句。

有时，非真实条件不是通过从句表示出来，而是通过介词短语、连接词或上下文表示出来。常见的可以引导虚拟条件的介词有：with, without, under, but for, for fear of 等，介词短语表示的虚拟条件相当于一个非真实条件从句。常见的可以用来引导虚拟条件的连接词有 or, but, but that, otherwise 等。

Without electricity（=If there were no electricity），there would be no modern industry.

But for the storm（= If it had not been for the storm），we should have arrived earlier.

He must be crazy, otherwise（=if he hadn't been crazy）he wouldn't have divorced her.

But that I caught her（=If I hadn't caught her），she would have fallen into the river.

2. 用于 as if 或 as though 引导的方式状语从句

	主句动词的形式	方式状语从句中谓语动词形式
表示与过去事实相反的情况	不限	had + 过去分词
表示与现在事实相反或现在实际上并不存在的情况	不限	动词过去式（were）
表示将来实现可能性不大的情况	不限	would/should/could/might + 动词原形

They treat me as though I were a stranger.

She looks as if she would cry.

【注意】as if 也可用于陈述语气。

He walks as if he is drunk.

It seems as if it is going to rain.

3. 用于目的状语从句

在 lest, for fear that, in case 引导的目的状语从句中可以使用虚拟语气，谓语动词形式为 "（should/might+）动词原形"。in case 引导的从句中，也可以使用陈述语气。

He ran away lest he（should/might）be seen.

She reminded him twice for fear that he（should/might）forget.

Take an umbrella with you in case it rains/（should/might）rain.

（二）虚拟语气在宾语从句中的用法

1. 用于表示要求、建议或愿望的动词后接的宾语从句

一些表示命令和要求的动词 command, demand, order, require, request, ask, urge 等、表示建议的动词 advice, insist, move, propose, recommend, suggest 等或表示愿望的动词 decide, desire, determine, intend, prefer 等后接的宾语从句中，要求使用虚拟语气形式，谓语动词形式为（should+）动词原形。

We suggested that the committee（should）not give up the plan.

He ordered that the letter（should）be mailed at once.

【注意】当 suggest 意为 "暗示，表明"，insist 意为 "坚持说，固执的声称" 时，后接的宾语从句要用陈述语气。

He still insists that he wasn't there at that time.

Are you suggesting that I'm not telling the truth?

2. 用于 wish 后接的宾语从句

动词 wish 后接的宾语从句中必须使用虚拟语气形式，if only 的用法与 wish 的用法完全相同，只是 if only 比 wish 表达更生动。

	主句中 wish 的形式	宾语从句中谓语动词形式
表示对过去情况的遗憾	不限	had + 过去分词 would/should/could/might + have+ 过去分词
表示对目前情况的遗憾	不限	动词过去式（were）
表示没有多大希望实现的将来愿望	不限	would/should/could/might + 动词原形 were + 现在分词

I wished I had not lost the chance.

He wishes that he were able to pass the final-exam.

I wish it were not raining tomorrow.

3. 用于 would rather/sooner/prefer/just as soon（that）后接的宾语从句

	主句中动词的形式	宾语从句中谓语动词形式
表示对过去情况的希望或委婉的责备	would sooner/rather/prefer would just as soon	had + 过去分词
表示对目前或将来情况的希望或委婉的责备	would sooner/rather/prefer would just as soon	动词过去式（were）

We would rather（that）it were winter now.

I would prefer（that）you did it now.

I would sooner（that）you had gone to the party last night.

4. 用于 imagine, suppose/supposing 后接的宾语从句

动词 imagine, suppose/supposing 后接的宾语从句要使用虚拟语气形式，表示一种猜想，通常是不可能发生的情况。表示对现在或将来的猜想，谓语动词用"过去式（were）"；表示对过去的猜想，谓语动词用"had+ 过去分词"。

Imagine that we were on an island now.

Supposing you had a million dollars, how would you spend it?

Suppose he had not taken those measures, what would have happened?

（三）虚拟语气在主语从句中的用法

1. 用于"It is + 形容词 + that…"句型

常见的形容词有 important, vital, necessary, essential, imperative, advisable, desirable, natural, better, urgent 等，谓语动词形式为"（should+）动词原形"。strange, amazing, odd, surprising 等用于该句型时，谓语动词形式为"should+ 动词原形"或"should have+ 过去分词"，表示说话人惊异、懊悔、失望等感情色彩。

It is necessary that he（should）be sent there at once.

It is amazing that he should have learnt so much in such a short time.

2. 用于"It is + 名词 + that…"句型

常见的名词有 pity, shame, wonder 等，谓语动词形式为"should+ 动词原形"或"should have+ 过去分词"，表示说话人惊异、懊悔、失望等感情色彩。

It is a pity that he should be so selfish.

It is a shame that she should have done such a thing.

3. 用于"It is + 过去分词 + that…"句型

常见的动词过去分词有 desired, suggested, proposed, requested, decided, advised 等，

谓语动词形式为"（should+）动词原形"。

It is advised that everyone（should）master at least one skill.

It was requested that every question（should）be answered.

（四）虚拟语气在表语从句和同位语从句中的用法

表示命令、要求、建议的名词，如：order, requirement, advice, plan, idea, suggestion, proposal, decision 等后接的表语从句或同位语从句中，要使用虚拟语气形式，谓语动词形式为"（should +）动词原形"。

Their decision was that the plan（should）be carried out next year.

My suggestion is that the problem（should）be settled as soon as possible.

Your advice that she（should）come next week is reasonable.

（五）虚拟语气在定语从句中的用法

用于"It is（about/high）time that…"句型中，从句中的谓语动词形式为动词过去式（were），意为"该是……的时候了"。

It is（high）time that you started working.

It is（about）time that you learnt to look after yourself.

专项练习题

1. This platform would fall down if all of you ＿＿ on it.

   A. stand   B. stood

   C. would stand   D. had stood

2. If I had time ＿＿ see that new movie.

   A. I'll   B. I may

   C. I shall   D. I'd

3. If you ＿＿ to see Mary, what would you tell her?

   A. are   B. are going

   C. have   D. were

4. Without water, there ＿＿ no plants.

   A. would have   B. would be

   C. were to be   D. were

5. If you ＿＿ in better health, we would have allowed you to join in the work.

   A. had been   B. were

C. should be   D. would be

6. If only we ____ a phone! I'm tired of queuing outside the public phone box.

     A. shall have   B. should have

     C. have   D. had

7. He was very busy yesterday; otherwise, he ____ to the meeting.

     A. would come   B. came

     C. would have come   D. should come

8. If I ____ harder at school, I would be sitting in a comfortable office now.

     A. worked   B. had worked

     C. were to work   D. were working

9. The business is risky. But ____, we would be rich.

     A. might we succeed   B. should we succeed

     C. would we succeed   D. could we succeed

10. ____ today, he would get there by Friday.

     A. Would he leave   B. Was he leaving

     C. Were he to leave   D. If he leaves

11. ____ his door number, I would have gone to visit him.

     A. If I knew   B. Had I known

     C. If I should know   D. Were I to know

12. Suppose you ____ the criminal the police are looking for.

     A. may be   B. were

     C. was   D. be

13. He looks as if he ____ ill for some time.

     A. had been   B. was

     C. is   D. be

14. ____ the fog, we should have reached our destination.

     A. Because of   B. In case of

     C. In spite of   D. But for

15. If only we ____ to their advice.

     A. listened   B. have listened

     C. had listened   D. should listen

16. Frankly, I'd rather you ____ anything about it for the time being.

     A. do   B. didn't do

     C. don't   D. won't do

17. I suggest that the students each _____ a plan for the summer vacation.

    A. would make   B. will make

    C. should make   D. made

18. I wish that we _____ with my brother when he flies to England next week.

    A. had gone   B. could go

    C. will go   D. are going

19. It is about time that something _____ to stop pollution.

    A. should do   B. were done

    C. would be done   D. did

20. It is a pity that he _____ so conceited.

    A. is   B. be

    C. was   D. should be

第十二节　非谓语动词

在英语中，一个简单句中只能有一个谓语动词，当句子需要其他动词来修饰或补充说明的时候，只能用非谓语动词形式，包括动词不定式、动名词和分词（包括现在分词和过去分词）。

一、非谓语动词的分类、构成和作用

分类	语法作用	构成		
		时态和语态	否定结构	复合结构
不定式	具有名词、副词和形容词的作用，可作除谓语以外的任何成分（主语、宾语、表语、定语、状语、宾语补足语）	to do → to be done to be doing → / to have done → to have been done	在非谓语形式前面加 not	for sb. to do sth.
动名词	具有名词的作用，可作表语、宾语补足语、定语、状语	doing → being done having done → having been done		sb.'s doing
现在分词	具有副词和形容词的作用，可作主语、宾语、表语、定语	doing → being done having done → having been done		
过去分词		done		

二、动词不定式的用法

（一）动词不定式作主语

常用 it 作形式主语，而将真正的主语后置。

To protect the environment is important for us.

=It's important for us to protect the environment.

1. It is + 形容词（名词）+for sb.+to do

用于该句型的形容词有 easy, difficult, hard, necessary, impossible, (un)necessary, (un)important 等，用来表示客观情况。

It is a great honor for us to be present at the party.

It is still a question for them how to get enough water.

2. It is + 形容词 +of sb.+to do

用于该句型的形容词有 careless, clever, considerate, foolish, good, honest, impolite, kind, lazy, naughty, nice, right, wrong, rude, silly, stupid, unwise, wise, generous 等，用来表示人物性格、特点。

It was very kind of him to help us.

It is generous of her to lend me so much money.

（二）动词不定式作宾语

序号	用法	例句
1	用在及物动词后面作宾语，常见的及物动词有：begin, choose, continue, decide, expect, fail, forget, help, hope, learn, manage, mean, need, offer, plan, prefer, pretend, promise, refuse, try, want, wish, determine, afford, agree, start, like, arrange, attempt, seek, tend, long, threaten, volunteer, wish 等	She promised to come at nine o'clock. They decided to put off the meeting till next week.
2	动词不定式作介词的宾语 ① "to do" 仅限于作 but 或 except 等少数介词的宾语。当 but 或 except 前有实义动词 do 的各种形式时，but 或 except 后面接不带 to 的动词不定式。当 but 或 except 前是其他动词时，but 或 except 后面接带 to 的动词不定式。 ② "疑问词 +to do" 结构作介词宾语，可用于任何介词	① Last night I did nothing but/except watch TV. I have no choice but /except to wait. ② I have no idea (about/of) what to do next. Every one has his own idea (of) how to do it.
3	it 代替不定式作形式宾语，常见动词：find, take, think, consider, suppose, feel, make 等	I find it very easy to read English every day. He thought it a great pity not to have invited her.

（三）动词不定式作宾语补足语

序号	用法	例句
1	不定式用在某些动词等之后作宾语补足语，常见动词有 ask, advise, allow, beg, cause, compel, command, direct, enable, encourage, expect, force, get, hate, help, inspire, intend, invite, instruct, lead, order, permit, persuade, press, remind, request, teach, tell, urge, want, warn, wish 等	I advised him to see a doctor at once. We warned her not to do that again.
2	省略 to 的不定式作宾语补足语： ①用在使役性动词 make, let, have 后面。 ②用于感官动词 see, hear, watch, notice, feel, observe, listen to, look at 等后面	I saw him enter the room. I have heard him speak about you often. I won't let you go alone.
3	动词 think, believe, suppose, know, feel, find, understand, declare 等后面要用 "to be+ 形容词（名词）" 结构作宾补，to be 可以省略，但 to have been 不可以省略	We know the book (to be) interesting. He was believed to have been foolish.

（四）动词不定式作表语

用来说明主语的内容，用来表示预定将要发生的动作或未来的可能性和假设。

My suggestion is to take measures at once.

（五）动词不定式作定语

多为后置定语，和所修饰的词有逻辑上的动宾、主谓及修饰等关系。

I want some paper to write on.

The next train to arrive was from Beijing.

I don't know the way to do it, either.

（六）动词不定式作状语

不定式在句中可以作目的状语、结果状语、原因状语等。

He went home (in order/so as)to see his mother.（目的状语）

She got up early in order/so as not to miss the first bus.（目的状语）

He lifted a rock only to drop it on his own feet.（结果状语）

He was so busy as to be unable to see anyone.（结果状语）

She burst into tears to hear the news.（原因状语）

（七）动词不定式的独立成分作状语

不定式的独立成分作状语时，表明说话人的态度。常用的独立成分有 to be exact, to be honest, to be frank with you, to be sure, to conclude, to begin/start with, to cut a long story short, to tell the truth, to sum up 等。

To tell you the truth, I know little about it.

To begin with, I don't like its style.

（八）"形容词 +to do"结构

"形容词 +to do"结构中，不定式逻辑主语是句子的主语。常见的形容词有 afraid, anxious, ashamed, careful, curious, determined, eager, fit, free, frightened, glad, keen, quick, ready, reluctant, slow, sorry, willing, bound, sure 等。

I am afraid to tell her about it.

She is always ready to help others.

Be careful not to catch cold.

（九）不定式符号 to 的省略

由 why 或 why not 引导的疑问句中省略不定式符号 to；在 had better, would rather, would rather...than, would sooner, would sooner...than, can't but, can't help but, might (just) as well 等后面省略不定式符号 to。

Why leave the door open?

Why not try again?

They would rather die than surrender.

You had better leave now.

Since she is angry, we might as well leave her alone.

三、动名词的用法

（一）动名词作主语

动名词作主语表示一般或抽象的多次行为，不与特定动作执行者联系在一起。

Saying is easier than doing.

Smoking is harmful to your health.

作主语时，有时用 it 作形式主语，动名词后置。常用于以下句型：

（1）It is + 名词 +doing，常见的名词有 no use, no good, fun, bore, a waste of time, a pity 等。

It is no use crying over spilt milk.

It's a waste of time arguing with him. He will not listen to you.

（2）It is+ 形容词 +doing，常见的形容词有 hard, difficult, nice, better, worthwhile, interesting, tiring, foolish, terrible, crazy, funny 等。

It is nice working/to work with you.

It was very difficult getting/to get everything ready in time.

It is worthwhile trying/to try again.

（二）动名词作宾语

序号	用法	例句
1	作动词宾语，常见用动名词作宾语的动词有 admit, anticipate, acknowledge, avoid, appreciate, allow, advise, bear, complete, consider, delay, deny, enjoy, endure, escape, excuse, explain, fancy, finish, forgive, favor, imagine, include, involve, keep, mention, mind, miss, pardon, practice, prevent, permit, quit, recall, recommend, reject, resent, resist, risk, suggest, tolerate, understand, cannot help, cannot stand, give up, put off 等	Why do you avoid meeting him? I cannot stand being treated like a beggar.
2	作介词或介词短语的宾语：look forward to, pay attention to, appeal to, admit to, confess to, contribute to, object to, amount to, take to, be used/accustomed to, be opposed to, be devoted to, in addition to 等短语中的 to 为介词，后接动名词作宾语	He left without saying good-bye to us. She is afraid of going out alone at night. I am looking forward to seeing you again.
3	it 代替动名词作形式宾语动名词作宾语	Do you consider it any good trying again? She found it no use arguing with him.

（三）动名词作表语

动名词作表语，说明主语的内容，表示一般或抽象的多次行为。

My hobby is collecting stamps.

What I am thinking now is going abroad.

（四）动名词作定语

动名词作定语要放在所修饰名词的前面，说明该名词的功能或用途。

drinking water　　washing machine

（五）动名词的其他结构

（1）have difficulty/trouble (in) doing，表示"做某事有困难"；have fun/pleasure/a good time (in) doing，表示"以做某事为乐"。

They have no difficulty finishing the work on time.

The children have fun playing football.

（2）spend/waste time/money/energy (in) doing，表示"花费（浪费）时间、金钱、精力做某事"。

He spent five days (in) working at the problem.

We mustn't waste time (in) arguing

（3）What/How about doing，用于提出建议或请求，意为"做……怎么样"或"做……

如何"。

What /How about having another cup of coffee?

What/How about leaving now?

（4）be busy (in) doing、busy oneself (in/with) doing，表示"忙着做某事"。

We are busy preparing for the final exam.

He is busying himself cooking the dinner.

（5）What is the use/good/point of doing，表示"做……也没有用"。

What is the use of persuading him?

What is the point of getting angry?

（6）do (some) + 动名词，表示"做……"。

She went to Hong Kong only to do some shopping.

On Sundays she usually helps her mother to do some washing.

（六）动名词作宾语和不定式作宾语的比较

（1）begin, start, continue, cease, neglect 接不定式或动名词作宾语，意义差别不大，但如果表示有意识地"开始或停止做某事"，多用动名词。

I began writing books in 1999.

At last they ceased talking.

It began to rain as soon as we got home.

（2）在 begin, start, continue 等后面时，或句子的时态为进行时态，只能用不定式。

I soon began to understand what was happening.

I'm beginning to cook the dinner.

（3）当主语为物或 it 时，want, need, require, deserve + doing = …to be done。

My car needs repairing/to be repaired.

The point deserves mentioning/to be mentioned.

（4）动词 love, like, hate, prefer, dislike 接不定式表示具体的或一次性的动作，接动名词表示一般的或抽象的多次行为。

Do you like playing/to play basketball?

I prefer listening/to listen to music.

Do you like having/to have a walk with me?

（5）动词 remember, forget, regret, mean, try, stop, go on 等后接不定式或动名词作宾语时，意义差别较大。

remember to do，意为"记住要去做某事"，表示动作尚未发生；

remember doing，意为"记得做过某事"，表示动作已经发生。

Please remember to post the letter.

I remember posting the letter.

forget to do，意为"忘记要去做某事"，表示动作尚未发生；

forget doing，意为"忘记做过某事"，表示动作已经发生。

Don't forget to feed the cat.

I forget seeing her.

regret to do，意为"遗憾要去做某事"，表示动作尚未发生；

regret doing，意为"后悔做过某事"，表示动作已经发生。

I regret to say I must leave tomorrow.

I regret not having told her earlier.

mean to do，意为"打算做某事"；

mean doing，意为"意味着"。

What do you mean to do?

His words mean refusing us.

try to do，意为"努力、设法做某事"；

try doing，意为"试着做某事"。

I will try to be here on time.

Try phoning his home number.

stop to do，意为"停下某事去做另一件事"；

stop doing，意为"停止做某事"。

He stopped to talk.

He stopped talking.

go on to do，意为"接着做另外的事"；

go on doing，意为"接着做同一件事"。

You can't go on working without a break.

After reading the book, he went on to do some writing.

四、现在分词和过去分词的用法

（一）现在分词和过去分词的区别

（1）在语态上，现在分词表示主动意义，过去分词表示被动意义。

the exploiting class 剥削阶级

the exploited class 被剥削阶级

（2）在时间上，现在分词表示正在进行的动作，过去分词表示已经完成的动作。

the developing country 发展中国家　　　the developed country 发达国家

the rising sun 正在升起的太阳　　the risen sun 升起来的太阳

（二）分词作定语

单个分词一般作前置定语；分词短语一般作后置定语。

The exciting experience made him sleepless.

Used cars are cheaper than new ones.

The matter being discussed was of great importance.

The fish caught yesterday was still alive.

（三）分词作状语

Not knowing English, he couldn't understand the film.（原因状语）

(Being) Tired and sleepy, she went to bed.（原因状语）

Turning to the left, you will see the post office.（条件状语）

Given another chance, I'll do it much better.（条件状语）

He sat in the sofa reading a newspaper.（伴随状语）

The boy walked down the hill, (being) followed by his dog.（伴随状语）

Her husband died, leaving her with five children.（结果状语）

Admitting what he has said, I still think he hasn't tried his best.（让步状语）

Hearing the news, he burst into tears.（时间状语）

Having done their homework, the students left the classroom.（时间状语）

【注意】before, after 后面不能直接接过去分词，要使用"being+ 过去分词"。

I waited ten minutes before being served.

The teenager ran away after being punished.

（四）分词独立成分作状语

现在分词一般式作状语，少数情况下，其逻辑主语与句子主语不一致，这时，分词形成独立成分，修饰整个句子。常见的独立成分有 broadly/generally/strictly speaking, talking/speaking of, judging from/by, considering 等。

Generally speaking, this film is not very interesting.

Judging from his accent, he must come from the Northeast.

Strictly speaking, you have no right to do that.

（五）分词作宾语补足语

（1）感官动词 see, observe, notice, watch, hear, smell, feel, find, listen to, catch 等，使役动词 set, get, leave, keep, have, make 等可以接分词作宾补。

He smelt something burning.

He found himself being followed by a stranger.

She still could not make herself understood in English.

（2）感官动词 +doing 和感官动词 +do 的区别。

"感官动词 +doing" 表示动作正在进行；"感官动词 +do" 表示动作已经完成。

She saw the man get on the bus.

She saw the man getting on the bus.

（3）have sb. do sth., have sb./sth. doing, have sth. done 的区别。

① have sb. do sth "让……做某事"，have 可以用 let, make 代替，往往表示一次性的具体动作，且强调动作已经完成或尚未发生。

I had John find me a house.

I'll have the gardener plant some trees.

② have sb./sth. doing "让……一直做某事"，have 可以用 keep 代替。

It was cold outside, we had the fire burning all the night.

③ have sth. done "使某事被做"，含被动意义。

Why don't you have your hair cut?

They are going to have their house painted.

专项练习题

1. When I went into the room, I found _____ in bed.

    A. him lying   B. he lying

    C. he lies   D. him was lying

2. Drivers shouldn't be allowed _____ after drinking.

    A. drive   B. driving

    C. to drive   D. to be driven

3. _____ energy, turn off the hot water after you take a shower.

    A. Save   B. Saving

    C. Saved   D. To save

4. Welcome to our school, ladies and gentlemen. _____, I'd like to introduce myself.

    A. To be honest   B. To my surprise

    C. To start with   D. To tell you the truth

5. _____ in the fields on a March afternoon, she could feel the warmth of spring.

    A. To walk   B. Walking

C. Walked   D. Having walked

6. The trees _____ in the storm have been moved off the road.

    A. to blow down   B. blown down

    C. blowing down   D. being blown down

7. Nick, would you mind _____ those old jeans? They look terrible.

    A. not to wear   B. not wear

    C. wearing not   D. not wearing

8. One of the difficulties we have _____ English is how to remember new words and expressions.

    A. to learn   B. learning

    C. learn   D. learned

9. If prices rise too high, the government has to do something _____ it.

    A. stop   B. stopped

    C. stopping   D. to stop

10. Since you are tired, you'd better _____ and have a good rest.

    A. stop to study   B. stop study

    C. stop studying   D. to stop to study

11. The book is well worth _____. I plan _____ one.

    A. read, to buy   B. reading, buying

    C. reading , to buy   D. to read, to buy

12. Mr. Wang does what he can _____ us improve our English.

    A. help   B. to help

    C. helping   D. helped

13. I saw Li Ming _____ near the river on my way home.

    A. plays   B. playing

    C. to play   D. played

14. This math problem is too difficult. Can you show me _____, George?

    A. what to work out   B. to work it out

    C. how to work it out   D. how to work out it

15. Teachers often tell us _____ in the river after school.

    A. don't swim   B. not swim

    C. not to swim   D. to not swim

16. The thief was noticed _____ the office building by the back door on the screen.

    A. enter   B. enter into

C. to enter   D. to enter into

17. Look! We can't cross the bridge. It ____ by some workers.

     A. repairs   B. is repaired

     C. is being repaired   D. is repairing

18. We went to the beach last Sunday, and we had great fun ____ volleyball.

     A. play   B. playing

     C. played   D. to play

19. Remember ____ the book to the library when you finish ____ it.

     A. to return, to read   B. returning, reading

     C. to return, reading   D. returning, to read

20. She used to ____ in the morning, but now she is used to ____ at night.

     A. read, read   B. read, reading

     C. reading, read   D. reading, reading

21. We can make a fire ____ the room warm so that we can chat for a while.

     A. to keep   B. keeping

     C. keep   D. kept

22. Jane's mother preferred ____ TV at home to ____ to the concert.

     A. to watch, go   B. watching, going

     C. watching, go   D. to watch, going

23. She reached the top of the hill and stopped ____ on a big rock.

     A. to have rested   B. resting

     C. to rest   D. rest

24. Do you know the boy ____ under the tree?

     A. lay   B. lain

     C. laying   D. lying

25. It's very important for us ____ English well.

     A. learn   B. learning

     C. to learn   D. learned

26. It is our duty ____ our hometown clean and beautiful. We must do something for it.

     A. to keep   B. keeps

     C. keeping   D. keep

27. Water Park is a good place ____.

     A. to have fun   B. have fun

     C. having fun   D. to have a fun

28. Kitty would rather _____ to the park than watch TV.

  A. to go   B. go

  C. going   D. goes

29. The boss made him work 14 hours a day. That means, he _____ work 14 hours a day.

  A. was made   B. made

  C. was making   D. was made to

30. The little boy pretended _____ when his mother came in.

  A. sleeping   B. asleep

  C. to asleep   D. to be asleep

31. Tom's mother is busy _____ breakfast for Tom.

  A. cook   B. to cook

  C. cooks   D. cooking

32. The assistant won't let you _____ the cinema if you haven't a ticket.

  A. enter   B. to enter

  C. entering   D. to entered

33. Some of the experiments _____ in the book are easy to perform.

  A. describing   B. to be described

  C. described   D. to describe

34. _____ in the fog, we were forced to spend two hours in the forest.

  A. To lose   B. Losing

  C. Lost   D. Having lost

35. It is no use his _____ there; the situation is hopeless now.

  A. to go   B. going

  C. having gone   D. to be going

36. Do you consider it any good _____ English in the morning?

  A. reading   B. to read

  C. to be read   D. reads

37. I regret _____ hard at school.

  A. not to have worked B. not have worked

  C. not having worked D. having not worked

38. Your flat needs _____. Would you like me _____ it for you?

  A. to clean, to do   B. cleaning, to do

  C. cleaning, doing   D. to be cleaned ... doing

39. He is beginning ____ his mistakes.

    A. see   B. to see

    C. seeing   D. seen

40. You should work instead of ____ TV.

    A. watch   B. you watching

    C. you watch   D. watching

41. Do you think the water is warm enough ____?

    A. go to swim   B. to go swimming

    C. for swim   D. to be swum

42. I was just about ____ the office when the phone rang.

    A. leaving   B. to leave

    C. to have left   D. to leaving

43. He meant ____ us about it, but he forgot to do so.

    A. telling   B. to tell

    C. having told   D. to have told

44. I'm very happy ____ a chance to visit your country.

    A. to be given   B. to be giving

    C. to give   D. giving

45. Did you notice the little boy ____ the candy and run away?

    A. taking   B. bring

    C. take   D. bringing

46. We would rather put the meeting off than ____ it without adequate preparation.

    A. to hold   B. hold

    C. holding   D. held

47. Curiously enough, she pretended ____ my name.

    A. to forget   B. to have forgotten

    C. to be forgotten   D. to have been forgotten

48. The lab ____ next year will be more advanced than the old one.

    A. built   B. being buil

    C. to be built   D. to build

49. He reached the airport exhausted only ____ that the plane had just taken off.

    A. learned   B. learn

    C. learning   D. to learn

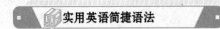

50. I spoke to him kindly _____ him.
   A. to not frighten   B. for not frightening
   C. in order to not frighten D. so as not to frighten

第二章 句子与特殊结构

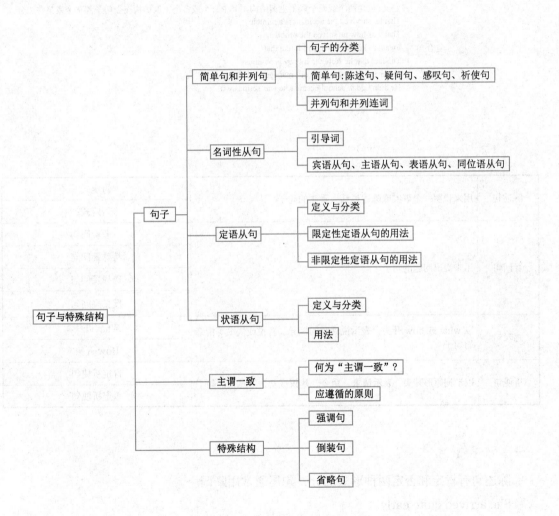

句子与特殊结构 —— 句子
- 简单句和并列句
  - 句子的分类
  - 简单句：陈述句、疑问句、感叹句、祈使句
  - 并列句和并列连词
- 名词性从句
  - 引导词
  - 宾语从句、主语从句、表语从句、同位语从句
- 定语从句
  - 定义与分类
  - 限定性定语从句的用法
  - 非限定性定语从句的用法
- 状语从句
  - 定义与分类
  - 用法
- 主谓一致
  - 何为"主谓一致"？
  - 应遵循的原则
- 特殊结构
  - 强调句
  - 倒装句
  - 省略句

第一节　简单句和并列句

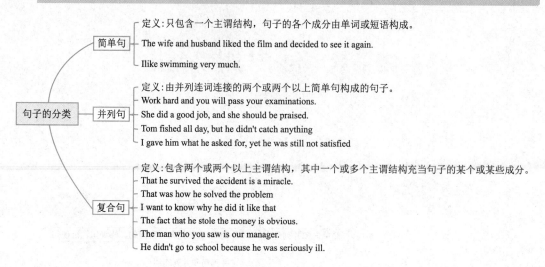

句子的分类

简单句
定义:只包含一个主谓结构,句子的各个成分由单词或短语构成。
The wife and husband liked the film and decided to see it again.
Ilike swimming very much.

并列句
定义:由并列连词连接的两个或两个以上简单句构成的句子。
Work hard and you will pass your examinations.
She did a good job, and she should be praised.
Tom fished all day, but he didn't catch anything
I gave him what he asked for, yet he was still not satisfied

复合句
定义:包含两个或两个以上主谓结构,其中一个或多个主谓结构充当句子的某个或某些成分。
That he survived the accident is a miracle.
That was how he solved the problem
I want to know why he did it like that
The fact that he stole the money is obvious.
The man who you saw is our manager.
He didn't go to school because he was seriously ill.

一、简单句

陈述句	用来说明一个事实或陈述说话人看法的句子	肯定式
		否定式
疑问句	用来提出问题的句子	一般疑问句
		特殊疑问句
		选择疑问句
		反义疑问句
感叹句	以 what 或 how 开头,表示说话时的惊异、喜悦或气愤等情绪的句子	What 开头
		How 开头
祈使句	以动词原形开头,表示请求、命令、建议或劝告等意义的句子	肯定祈使句
		否定祈使句

（一）陈述句

陈述句有肯定和否定两种形式之分,句尾通常用降调。

She arrived quite early.

She didn't answer the stranger's question.

（二）疑问句

1. 一般疑问句

以 be 动词、助动词或情态动词开头，用 yes 或 no 回答。一般疑问句的句尾通常用升调。

Do you speak English?   —Yes, I do. / No, I don't.

Will you accept his invitation?   —Yes, I will. /No, I won't.

Didn't I tell you to come early?

Can't you walk a little faster?

2. 特殊疑问句

以特殊疑问词开头，后接一般疑问句的句子。特殊疑问句句尾用降调。

如果特殊疑问句中加入一般疑问句形式的插入语，如 did you say, can you guess, do you think/suppose/believe 等，则特殊疑问句使用陈述语气，不可倒装。

What's happened?

Who are responsible for the project?

Who can you guess is in charge of the project?

Whom did you think I should see first?

3. 选择疑问句

以 be 动词、助动词或情态动词形式开头，给出两个或两个以上可能的选择，各部分用 or 连接起来的句子叫作选择疑问句。or 之前的部分要用升调，or 之后的部分用降调。

Do you work in a hospital ↗ or in a school? ↘

4. 反义疑问句

（1）构成：由陈述句和一个简短的一般疑问句组成，中间以 "," 隔开。

肯定陈述句 + 否定疑问句（be 动词 / 助动词 / 情态动词的否定形式要缩写）

否定陈述句 + 肯定疑问句（be 动词 / 助动词 / 情态动词 + 主语）

疑问句的主语通常和陈述句的主语一致，但需为人称代词。

They work hard, don't they?

She was ill yesterday, wasn't she?

You didn't go, did you?

He can't ride a bike, can he?

（2）特殊句式：

① 陈述部分是 I am... 时，反义疑问句用 aren't I?

I'm working hard now, aren't I?

I'm not sleeping, am I?

② 陈述句部分的主语是 this/that 时，反义疑问句的主语用 it/they, these/those。

This is a plane, ins't it?

③ 当陈述句是 there be 句型时，简短的问句用 be there?

④ 当祈使句部分含有以下否定意义的词时，few（极少），little（极少），seldom（极少），hardly（几乎不），never，not，no，no one，nothing，none，too...to... 句型，其反义疑问句需用肯定结构。

⑤ 当陈述句部分带有表示否定意义的前缀构成的词，反义疑问句用否定结构。

⑥ 若陈述句中含有 have/has：

➢ 如果 have/has 是表示完成时的助动词，反义疑问句借助 have/has。

➢ 如果 have/has 是实义动词，表"拥有"的意义，反义疑问句可借助助动词，也可用 have/has。

➢ 如果 have/has 是"吃、喝"的意义，反义疑问句需借助助动词。

⑦ 陈述句部分有 had better 时，后面的简短问句要用 had。

⑧ 祈使句的反义疑问句：

➢ 当陈述句是肯定祈使句时，反义疑问句为 won't you?/will you?

Open the door, won't you?/will you?

➢ 当陈述句是否定祈使句时，反义疑问句用 will you。

Don't close the window, will you?

➢ 当陈述句是 Let's... 时，反义疑问句用 shall we；若陈述句是 Let us... 反义疑问句用 will you。

Let's go home, shall we?

Let us help you, will you?

（三）感叹句

1. what 引导的感叹句：what 用来修饰名词

What beautiful flowers they are!

What a big room（it is）!（=How big a room it is!）

2. how 引导的感叹句：how 用来修饰形容词、副词或动词

How clever a boy he is!（=What a clever boy he is!）

How time flies!

（四）祈使句

1. Do 型祈使句

Stand up.

Come here, please.

否定句：Don't + 动词原形

Don't stand up.

Don't close the door.

2. Be 型祈使句：Be + adj./n.

Be quiet.

Be careful.

否定句：Don't be quiet.

Don't be careful.

3. Let 型祈使句：Let sb. / sth. do sth.

Let me/him open the door.

Let the kite fly high.

Let us watch TV.（不包括听者）

Let's watch TV.（包括听者）

二、并列句和并列连词

（一）并列句

由并列连词连接起来的两个或两个以上的简单句组成的句子叫作并列句。其构成为：简单句 + 并列连词 + 简单句。

（二）常见的并列连词

1. 表示顺承、并列、递进关系的连词及并列句

and "和"；both…and… "……和……两个都"；as well as "也"；not only…but also "不但……而且……"等。

My father bought me a present, and I like it very much.

2. 表示转折或对比关系的连词及并列句

but "但是"；yet "然而"；while "而"。

Lucy likes red while Lily likes white.

3. 表示选择关系的连词及并列句

either…or… "要么……要么……"，连接主语时，动词与靠近它的主语在人称、数上保持一致，即 "就近原则"。or "或者"，还可以表示 "否则"。

Study hard, or you'll fail the exam.

4. 表示因果关系的连词及并列句

so "因此、所以"，for "因为"，表示因果关系。

Kate was ill so she didn't go to school.

I have to stay up late, for I have lots of homework to do.

5. and 和 or 用于否定句的区别

① 当列举成分是主语，又在否定词之前，用 and 连接；当列举成分在否定词之后，用 or 构成完全否定。

Lucy and Lily can't speak Chinese.

I can't sing or dance.

② 在否定句中，如果所连接的两部分都有否定词，那么用 and, 不用 or。

There is no water and no air on the moon.

③ 在否定句中，without 之后如果有列举成分，用 and 连接构成完全否定；在肯定句中，without 之后的列举成分要用 or 连接才能构成完全否定。

Man can't live without air and water.

=Man will die without air or water.

专项练习题

1. _____ wake up your sister, Ben. She needs a good rest.

   A. Don't   B. Doesn't

   C. Aren't   D. Can't

2. _____ important it is for kids to imagine freely.

   A. What   B. What a

   C. What an   D. How

3. _____ kind and helpful to the people around us, and we will make the world a nicer place to live in.

   A. Be   B. Being

   C. To be   D. Been

4. —Will you join us for dinner?

   —_____.

   A. Do, I won't   B. Yes, with pleasure

   C. Yes, please   D. Yes, help yourself

5. —Do you mind if I sit here?

   — _____. It's for Mr Green.

   A. Not at all   B. Never mind

   C. Better not   D. Of course not

6. —Is he a teacher or a policeman?

    A. Yes, he is   B. No, he isn't

    C. A teacher   D. Yes, a teacher

7. —Can you play table tennis ____ basketball?

    —I can play table tennis.

    A.and   B. but

    C. or   D. so

8. —____ does your father go to see your grandmother?

    —Once a month.

    A.How long   B. How soon

    C. How often   D. How far

9. Nobody says a word about the accident, ____?

    A. is he   B. doesn't he

    C. do they   D. don't they

10. Hundreds of people lost their lives in the accident, ____ they?

    A. don't   B. didn't

    C. do   D. did

11. You had one of your teeth pulled out yesterday, ____?

    A. had you   B. didn't you

    C. did it   D. didn't it

12. What a lovely day, ____?

    A. doesn't it   B. isn't it

    C. shan't it   D. hasn't it

13. Nothing he did was right, ____?

    A. did he   B. was it

    C. didn't it   D. was he

14. She must have arrived there yesterday, ____?

    A. have she   B. must she

    C. didn't she   D. mustn't she

15. There used to be a post office behind the park, ____?

    A. didn't there   B. used there

    C. usedn't it   D. didn't it

16. He must be in the library now, ____?

    A. doesn't he   B. mustn't he

    C. needn't he   D. isn't he

17. My sister often needs help with her study, ____?

    A. need she   B. needn't she

    C. does she   D. doesn't she

18. Let's go swimming, ____?

    A. aren't we   B. shall we

    C. will you   D. won't we

19. He ought to have looked after his father, ____?

    A. oughtn't he   B. ought he not he

    C. oughtn't he to   D. oughtn't to be

20. None of the pupils attended the sports meet, ____?

    A. did they   B. do they

    C. didn't they   D. don't they

21. Everyone is here, ____?

    A. isn't it   B. isn't she

    C. aren't they   D. aren't you

22. There is little juice in the glass, ____?

    A. is there   B. isn't there

    C. is it   D. isn't it

23. ____some of this juice. Perhaps you'll like it.

    A. Trying   B. Try

    C. To try   D. Having tried

24. Let him alone, ____?

    A. will we   B. won't we

    C. will you   D. do you

25. ____ me the truth, or I won't let you leave here.

    A. Tell   B. To tell

    C. Telling   D. Told

26. ____ hard and you'll make progress in English.

    A. Work   B. To work

    C. Working   D. Worked

27. ____ good time we had at the party last night.

    A. What   B. How

    C. What a   D. How a

28. ____ day it is!

    A. What a lovely   B. How windy

    C. What a rainy   D. How lovely

29. ____ clever the girl is!

    A. How   B. What

    C. What a   D. How a

30. ____ music she is playing!

    A. What nice   B. How nice

    C. What a nice   D. How nice a

31. It's not always safe to pay over the Internet, ____ you should be careful.

    A. so   B. after

    C. became   D. as soon as

32. Hold your dream, ____ you might regret some day.

    A. and   B. or

    C. but   D. so

33. Jane, hurry up! ____ we can't arrive there on time.

    A. Or   B. So

    C. But   D. And

34. When you're tired, you can get close to the nature ____ you'll feel relaxed in the beauty all round.

    A. or   B. and

    C. but   D. while

35. Betty kept silent at first ____ soon she joined the other girls, chatting and laughing.

    A. so   B. but

    C. because   D. or

第二节 名词性从句

一、名词性从句的引导词

连接词	that, if, whether
疑问代词	who, whom, whose, what, which
	whoever, whomever, whatever, whichever
疑问副词	where, when, why, how

1. 连接词 that, if, whether 的用法

（1）that 本身无意义，在表语从句和宾语从句中可以省略；if 和 whether 意为"是否"，引导的从句表示"两种可能性居其一"，不能省略。

That he survived the accident is a miracle.

The problem is（that）we can't get there early enough.

I don't know whether/if he will attend the meeting.

（2）that 和 whether 可以引导所有名词性从句。if 只能引导宾语从句和主语从句，在引导宾语从句时，if 和 whether, whether…or（not）和 if…or（not）可以互换使用。在引导主语从句时，whether 可以位于句首，if 不可以位于句首。

I don't care whether/if you come or not.

Please try to find out whether/if he is at home or at the office.

Whether she comes or not makes no difference.

It is doubtful whether/if he is coming.

（3）动词 wonder 接 whether 或 if 引导的宾语从句时，意为"想知道……"，后接 that 引导的宾语从句时，意为"纳闷"。

I wonder whether/if he did it.

I wonder that he did it.

（4）动词 doubt 接 whether 或 if 引导的宾语从句，意为"不知道，怀疑"，接 that 引导的宾语从句，意为"不信"。

I doubt whether/if she will come.

I doubt that she will come.

I don't doubt that she will come.

2. 疑问代词 who, whom, whose, which 的用法

who, whom, whose, which, what 在句中既起引导从句的作用，又作主语、宾语或定语

等成分。

Who will do it hasn't been decided.

He asked whom I borrowed the money from.

I want to know whose car it is.

What follows is doubtful.

I want to know what happened.

That is exactly what he told me.

3. 疑问代词 whatever, whoever, whomever, whichever 的用法

引导名词性从句时，whatever, whoever, whomever, whichever 在句中起到"先行词 + that…"的双重作用，表示泛指的意义。

（1）whatever = anything that 或 any…that，在从句中作主语、宾语或定语等。

Whatever/What is worth doing should be done well.

We will be grateful for whatever amount you can afford.

（2）whoever = anyone who，在从句中作主语；whomever = anyone whom，在从句中作宾语。

Whoever makes mistakes must correct them.

He will give the book to whomever he likes.

（3）whichever = any（…）that/who，在从句中作主语、宾语或定语等。

You can take whichever room you prefer.

Please delete whichever is not appropriate.

4. 疑问副词 where, when, why, how 的用法

疑问副词 when, where, why, how 在句中既起引导从句作用，又作时间状语、地点状语、原因状语和方式状语。

When the meeting will begin is not decided.

That is where I used to live.

I didn't know why she didn't come.

The question is how we can get there on time.

二、名词性从句的种类

名词性从句	宾语从句	宾语从句可以作动词、介词或形容词的宾语
	主语从句	通常作整个句子的主语
	表语从句	通常放在 be 动词的后面
	同位语从句	同位语从句说明所修饰的名词的内容

（一）宾语从句

1. 宾语从句的时态

（1）如果主句是现在的某种时态（包括一般现在时、现在进行时、现在完成时），那么宾语从句的时态可根据实际情况而定。

I remember he gave me a book yesterday.

He has told me that he'll leave for Hangzhou tomorrow.

（2）如果主句是过去的某种时态（包括一般过去时、过去进行时）那么宾语从句一般要用过去的某种时态（包括一般过去时、过去进行时、过去将来时、过去完成时）。

He told me that he would take part in the high jump.

（3）如果宾语从句表示的是客观事实或真理，即使主句是过去时，从句也要用一般现在时态。

He told me that the earth is round.

2. 宾语从句的否定转移

当主句的主语是第一人称，谓语动词是 think, believe, suppose 等时，要将宾语从句的否定词转移到主句中。

I don't think he will come with you.

3. 宾语从句的语序

宾语从句的语序要用陈述句语序。当把两个独立的句子连成一个含有宾语从句的复合句时，要特别注意从句的语序，要按照主语、谓语的顺序。

Do you know what Kate's e-mail address?

4. 直接引语与间接引语

（1）引号中是陈述句。

① says → says，says to → tells。

② 去掉逗号、引号，用 that 连接，that 不翻译，可省略。

③ 变人称：一随主，二随宾，第三人称不更新。

Peter says，"I am having my lunch."　　　→ Peter says that he is having his lunch.

Bob says to Mary，"I will help you."　　　→ Bob tells Mary that he will help her.

Bob says，"I need you."　　　→ Bob says that he need me.

He says，"Mary is nice."　　　→ He says that Mary is nice.

（2）引号中是一般疑问句。

① says/says to → asks。

② 去掉逗号、引号，用 if 连接，if 意为"是否"，不可省略。

③ 将一般疑问句变回陈述句。

Did you go…?　　　→ you want…

Has he finished…?	→ he has finished…
Does your mother like…?	→ your mother likes…
Will she go…?	→ she will go…
Can I help you?	→ I can help you.
Peter says to Mary, "Are you tired?"	→ Peter asks Mary if she is tired.
He says, "Are you doing your homework?"	→ He asks if I am doing my homework.

（3）引号中是特殊疑问句。

① says / says to → asks。

② 去掉逗号、引号，用特殊疑问词连接，译成特殊疑问词本身的含义，不可省略。

③ 如果引号中的句子是特殊疑问词 + 一般疑问句构成，则将一般疑问句变成陈述句，否则不变。

Mary says to Peter, "Who do you like?"	→ Mary asks Peter who he likes.
Mary says to Peter, "Who likes you?"	→ Mary asks Peter who likes him.
He asks Bob, "Where are you going?"	→ He asks Bob where he is going.

（4）引号中是肯定 / 否定祈使句。

根据语气的不同转换为：

tell sb. to do sth./tell sb. not to do sth.

ask sb. to do sth./ask sb. not to do sth.

order sb. to do sth./order sb. not to do sth.

He says, "Tommy, to out."	→ He tells/orders Tommy to go out.
She says to Bob, "Do it for me."	→ She asks Bob to did it for her.
He says, "Tom, don't open the window."	→ He tells Tom not to open the window.

（二）主语从句

1. 大多数主语从句都可以用 it 作形式主语，常见 it 作形式主语结构有以下几种

（1）It is + 名词 +that…

It is a pity that…	遗憾的是……
It is a fact…	事实是……
It is no wonder…	……不足为奇
It is common knowledge that…	……是常识……

（2）It is + 形容词 + that…（从句不可置于句首）

It is obvious that…	……显而易见
It is fortunate that…	幸运的是……
It is natural that…	很自然……

It is possible that…	很可能……
It is unlikely that…	不可能……
It is strange that…	奇怪的是……

（3）It + 动词 + that…（从句不可置于句首）。

It seems that…	似乎……
It appears…	看来……
It turned out that…	结果……
It happened that…	碰巧……

（4）It is + 过去分词 +that…

It is well known that…	众所周知……
It is not decided that…	……尚未决定
It is said that…	据说……
It is reported that…	据报道……
It is recorded that…	据记载……
It is estimated that…	据估计……
It is generally believed/thought/supposed that…	普遍认为……

（5）其他形式。

It must be pointed out that…	必须指出……
It has been proved that…	已证明……
It doesn't matter…	……是无关紧要的
It makes no difference…	……毫无区别
It suddenly struck/occurred to me that…	我突然想到 …

2. what, whatever, whoever, whichever 引导的主语从句不能用 it 作形式主语

What he said is not true.

Whoever says that is a liar.

（三）表语从句

除 if 外，其余所有关联词都可引导表语从句。"It / This / That is / was because…" 结构中的 because 也可以用来引导表语从句。

It seems as if/that it is going to rain.

That was how he solved the problem.

This book is just what I have been looking for.

Why didn't you phone me last night? ——（It was）Because I didn't want to disturb you.

（四）同位语从句

同位语从句所修饰的名词有 belief, fact, idea, plan, doubt, news, information, evidence, discovery, decision, opinion, truth, thought, possibility, suggestion, order, promise, statement 等，一般由连接词 that 引导，that 不可省略。

The news that he failed the exam was disappointing.

The fact that he stole the money is obvious.

We are familiar with the idea that all matter consists of atoms.

The suggestion that she should do it again is not accepted.

专项练习题

1. This morning my mother asked me ____.

   A. why he is not here

   B. how did my brother do it

   C. what time it was

   D. what Judy did over the weekend

2. —What did he say just now?

   —He asked me ____.

   A. when did the Exhibition open

   B. when the Exhibition open

   C. when the Exhibition opened

   D. when does the Exhibition open

3. No one knows ____ in fifty years.

   A. what will our life be like

   B. what is our life like

   C. what our life will be like

   D. what our life is like

4. Who can tell me ____ at the meeting?

   A. what he said

   B. he said what

   C. what did he say

   D. how he said

5. Professor Nelson wanted to know ____.

   A. when would the conference begin

   B. when the conference would begin

   C. when will the conference begin

   D. when the conference will begin

6. For a long time nobody understood ____ food went bad.

   A. what

   B. when

   C. that

   D. why

7. ____ I can't understand is ____ he wants to change his mind.

   A. That, that

   B. Which, how

   C. What, that

   D. What, why

8. It _____ that space is limitless.

    A. believes

    B. was generally believed

    C. believed

    D. is generally believed

9. Scientists have reached the conclusion _____ the temperature on the earth is getting higher and higher.

    A. when

    B. but

    C. for which

    D. that

10. _____ knowledge is power is a famous saying known to all.

    A. What

    B. How

    C. That

    D. Why

11. _____ this material can be used in our factory has not been studied yet.

    A. Which

    B. What

    C. That

    D. Whether

12. I never doubt _____ it is true.

    A. whether

    B. if

    C. that

    D. what

13. The music was terrible. That's _____ they left the party.

    A. how

    B. why

    C. what

    D. because

14. Do you know _____?

    A. when does the movie start

    B. if does the movie start

    C. what time the movie starts

    D. what time starts the movie

15. Do you remember where _____ my watch?

    A. have I put

    B. I have put

    C. have put I

    D. put I

16. I have some tickets for the basketball match. I wonder _____.

    A. where you buy the tickets

    B. why you like to go there

    C. if you'd like to come along

    D. when you watch the match

17.The teacher is already standing here. Do you know when she _____?

    A. comes

    B. came

    C. is coming

    D. was coming

18. I don't know _____.

    A. how often he visits his grandparents

    B. how soon will he come back

C. how many students are there in his class

D. how long is the bridge

19. I don't understand ____ such a silly question in class yesterday.

    A. why John asks   B. why John asked

    C. why is John asking   D.why did John ask

20. —The light in his room is still on. Do you know ____?

    —In order to prepare for the coming exam.

    A. If he works hard   B. why he stays up so late

    C. why is he so busy   D. when he will stop working

第三节　定语从句

一、定语从句的定义与分类

（一）定义

（1）是指一类由关系词引导的从句，因这类从句的句法功能多是作定语，所以称为定语从句。

（2）先行词：定语从句所修饰的名词或代词。

（3）关系词：连接主句和从句，并在从句中作一定成分。

The man who lives next to us is a policeman.

先行词：the man

关系词：who

从句：who lives next to us

主句：The man is a policeman.

（二）分类

根据定语从句与先行词的语义关系，分为限定性定语从句和非限定性定语从句。

二、限定性定语从句

限定性定语从句紧跟先行词并和先行词关系密切，缺少了它，句子意思不完整。在翻译成汉语时应把整个从句置于先行词之前。常见限定性定语从句的引导词如下所示：

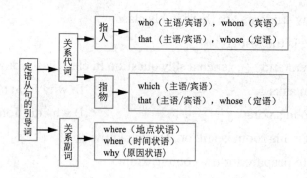

（一）关系代词

1. who

先行词为人，在从句中可作主语或宾语。

He is the person who I met yesterday.

He is the person who met me yesterday.

The girl who I like is Mary.

The girl who likes me is Mary.

2. whom

先行词为人，在从句中作宾语。

He is the boy whom（who）I like.

He is the person whom（who）I met yesterday.

3. which

先行词为物，在从句中作主语或宾语。

I bought the house which I like.

I bought the dress which is in the window.

The pen which you gave me is in my schoolbag.

4. that

先行词可以是人或物，在从句中可作主语或宾语。

5. whose

先行词为人或物，在从句中作定语，后面直接加名词。

He is the boy whose father is a teacher.

I bought the house whose kitchen is large.

（二）关系代词的特殊用法

1. 当关系代词在从句中作宾语时，通常可以省略

She is the girl who（whom）I like.

She is the girl I like.

2. 定语从句的关系代词本身没有单复数，当关系代词作主语时，谓语动词的单复数形式取决于先行词

He is the person who often helps me.

They are the persons who often help me.

He is one of the persons who often help me.

He is the only one of the persons who often helps me.

3. 当关系代词在从句中作介词的宾语时，介词不可省略，但介词可以提到关系代词前，此时只能用"介词 +which/ 介词 +whom"

I want to see the film which you are talking about.

I want to see the film about which you are talking.

He is the boy who you are looking for.

He is the boy for whom you are looking.

4. whose + 名词可转换为"of which/whom+the+ 名词"或"the+ 名词 +of which/whom"

He is the teacher whose eyes are big.

= He is the teacher the eyes of whom are big.

= He is the teacher of whom the eyes are big.

I like the house whose windows are clean.

= I like the house of which the windows are clean.

= I like the house the windows of which are clean.

5. 先行词指物，只能用 that 的情况

（1）先行词中既有人又有物。

I've never heard of the people and things that you talked about just now.

（2）先行词前面有序数词或形容词最高级修饰。

This is the best book that I have ever read.

（3）主句是 which/who 开头的特殊疑问句。

Which is the book that you bought yesterday?

（4）先行词前面有 the only, the very, the last, all, few, little, no, any, much 等词修饰。

This is the only book that I can find.

（5）当先行词是 all, little, much, none, everything, anything, nothing 等指物的不定代词。先行词为 something 时，多用 which 引导定语从句。

Tom told his mother all that had happened.

Please just tell me anything（that）you know about the accident.

He held in his hand something which resembled a letter.

6. as 引导限定性定语从句时，常用于 the same … as 和 such … as 结构中，既指人也指物，在引导的从句中作主语、宾语、表语

（1）用于 such … as 结构中。

Such people as were chosen by him were reliable.

Such books as I have read are classical works.

I've never seen such an honest man as he is.

This book is not such as I expect.（=This is not such a book as I expect.）

（2）用于 the same … as 结构中，表示"同类不同物"的意义。

This is the same watch as I lost.

I'd like to use the same tool as is used here.

（3）the same… 后面也可以接 that 引导的定语从句，此时 the same 相当于 the very，表示"同类同物"的意义。如果先行词表示抽象事物，则 as, that 引导的定语从句没有这种区别。

She is wearing the same coat that I lost several days ago.

She is wearing the same coat as I lost several days ago.

She told me the same story as/that she had told you.

（三）关系副词

1. when

先行词为表示时间的名词，如：day, time, era, age 等。在引导的从句中作时间状语，相当于 at/in/on/during which。

Do you remember the day（when/that/on which）they were married?

I can't remember the time（when/that/at which）she left.

They put off the sports meet till Friday, when/on which the weather may be better.

2. where

（1）先行词为表示地点的名词，如：place, factory, country, city 等。在引导的从句中作地点状语，相当于 at/in/on which。

That's the place（where/that/in which）he was born.

Here is the office（where/that/ at which）he works.

（2）先行词为表示"情况、方面"的名词，如 case, situation, conditions, stage 等，相当于 under/at which，意为"在……情况下"。

He had to face the conditions where/under which pressure was heavy.

This is a job where/from which you can learn something.

（3）where 可以和介词 from 连用，先行词为一个介词短语。from+ where 结构在意义

上相当于 and from there。

She stood near the window, from where she could see the church.

He hid himself under the bed, from where he could hear what they were talking.

3. why

先行词为表示原因的名词 reason。从句中作原因状语，相当于 for which。

That is reason(why/that)I did it.

The reason(why/that)he died was lack of medical care.

三、非限定性定语从句

非限定性定语从句通常要用逗号与先行词隔开，有时相当于一个并列句，起补充说明作用，有时在意义上相当于一个状语从句，缺少了它，句子意思仍然完整。

常见非限定性定语从句的引导词：

1. who, whom, whose

Our guide, who was a Canadian, was an excellent cook.

Mr. Smith, from whom I have learned a lot, is a famous scientist.

The boy, whose father is an engineer, studies very hard.

2. which

Which 在非限定性定语从句中所指代和修饰的可以是主句中的名词、短语、其他从句或整个句子，在从句中作主语、宾语或表语。

The apple trees, which I planted three years ago, have not borne any fruit.

She was very patient towards the children, which her husband was seldom was.

He said that he had never seen her before, which was not true.

In the presence of so many people he was little nervous, which was understandable.

3. when/where

He will put off the picnic until May 1st, when he will be free.

They went to London, where they lived for six months.

4. as

as 引导非限定性定语从句时，代替整个主句，表示一种附加说明，可以位于句首、句中或句尾，通常译为"正如……一样"或"正像……一样"。as 引导的非限定性定语从句在用法上往往相当于一个主语从句或宾语从句。

China, as we know, is rich in natural resources.

Children, as is always the case, love their mother.

He became crazy, as many could see.

as 引导的非限定性定语从句时常见短语：

as is well known 众所周知　　　as is often the case 情况常常如此
as may be imagined 可以想象得出　　as often happens 这种情况常常发生
as has been said before 如前所述　　as has been pointed out 正如已经指出的
as is hoped 正如所希望的　　　as is supposed/anticipated 如所预料的

专项练习题

1. Did you find the notebook ＿＿＿ Jim had given me for my birthday?
　A. who　　　　　　　　B. whom
　C. which　　　　　　　D. whose

2. That's all ＿＿＿ I have seen and heard.
　A. which　　　　　　　B that
　C. where　　　　　　　D. what

3. He never reads anything ＿＿＿ is not worth reading.
　A. that　　　　　　　　B. as
　C. who　　　　　　　　D. which

4. The man ＿＿＿ coat is black is waiting at the gate.
　A. who's　　　　　　　B. whose
　C. that　　　　　　　　D. of which

5. The police caught the man ＿＿＿ stole my handbag.
　A. he　　　　　　　　　B. that
　C. whom　　　　　　　D. which

6. The girl ＿＿＿ is reading under the tree ＿＿＿ my sister.
　A. which, is　　　　　　B. whom, was
　C. who, is　　　　　　　D. who, was

7. George was an English teacher ＿＿＿ loved climbing.
　A. who　　　　　　　　B. whom
　C. he　　　　　　　　　D. which

8. This is the bag ＿＿＿ my mother bought yesterday.
　A. that　　　　　　　　B. who
　C. whom　　　　　　　D. this

9. The man ＿＿＿ lives next to us is my English teacher.
　A. who　　　　　　　　B. whom
　C. which　　　　　　　D. /

10. The girl ＿＿ you saw in the street is Mary.

　　A. that

　　B. which

　　C. whose

　　D. /

11. The only language ＿＿ is easy to learn is the mother tongue.

　　A. which

　　B. that

　　C. who

　　D. /

12. The girl handed everything ＿＿ she had picked up in the street to the police.

　　A. which

　　B. in which

　　C. that

　　D. all

13. Please show me the book ＿＿ you bought yesterday.

　　A. which

　　B. whom

　　C. whose

　　D. this

14. The man and the horse ＿＿ fell into the river were drowned.

　　A. which

　　B. who

　　C. that

　　D. of which

15. I like to make friends with the kind of person ＿＿ is honest and friendly.

　　A. whom

　　B. who

　　C. which

　　D. what

16. What is the matter? I can't find the book ＿＿ I like best.

　　A. it

　　B. what

　　C. that

　　D. they

17. I'll never forget the words ＿＿ my teacher said to me.

　　A. who

　　B. whom

　　C. which

　　D. whose

18. She lives in a house ＿＿ windows face south.

　　A. that

　　B. who

　　C. which

　　D. whose

19. That was all the money ＿＿ I had.

　　A. which

　　B. that

　　C. whom

　　D. whose

20. Look at the boy and his dog ＿＿ are coming this way.

　　A. who

　　B. which

　　C. that

　　D. whom

21. This was the place _____ last year.

    A. which we visited   B. where we visited

    C. when we visited   D. in which we visited

22. There are no children _____ love their parents.

    A. that do not   B. who does not

    C. that   D. who

23. The days _____ they had been looking forward to _____ at last.

    A. which, came   B. that, come

    C. when, coming   D. when, came

24. The building _____ we built last year is very tall.

    A. where   B. what

    C. that   D. when

25. The little boy likes reading those books _____ beautiful pictures in them.

    A. which has   B. which have

    C. that having   D. that has

26. This is the most difficult book _____.

    A. what I have ever read   B. which I have ever read

    C. I have ever read it   D. that I have ever read

27. Do you know the student _____?

    A. whom Tom often plays with   B. with whom Tom often play

    C. Tom often play   D. with who Tom often play

28. I am interesting in _____ you have told me.

    A. which   B. all that

    C. that   D. everything of which

29. There is a mountain _____ the top is always covered with snow.

    A. of that   B. of which

    C. its   D. which

30. The reason _____ Jane didn't arrive on time was not clear.

    A. which   B. why

    C. what   D. that

31. I can still remember the classroom _____ I used to study ten years ago.

    A. when   B. that

    C. where   D. which

32. This is the village _____ he used to live.

    A. which   B. where

    C. that   D. when

33.The world _____ we live is made up of matter.

    A. on which   B. of which

    C. at which   D. in which

34. We have not decided the date _____ we shall start our holidays.

    A. that   B. when

    C. which   D. where

35. The tree, _____ is in front of the house, is very old.

    A. which   B. that

    C. whose   D. as

36. Simon's brother, _____ lives in London, is an architect.

    A. who   B. whom

    C. whose   D. that

37. The weather turned out to fine, _____ was more than we could expect.

    A. which   B. what

    C. it   D. that

38.My grandmother, _____ cooks very well, is very kind.

    A. who   B. that

    C. whom   D. she

39.I have a lot of friends, _____ studying abroad now.

    A. some of them is   B. some of them are

    C. some of whom is   D. some of whom are

40. Our teacher, _____ you met just now, is very strict with us.

    A. which   B. whom

    C. that   D. he

第四节 状语从句

一、状语从句的定义与分类

（一）定义

在复合句中修饰主句或主句中的动词等，由从属连词引导。与主句连接，位于句首时，常用逗号与主句分开；位于句末时，前面一般不用逗号。

（二）分类

分类	引导词
时间状语从句	when/while/as, before, after, since, not…until, as soon as，the moment/minute/instant, immediately, directly, every time, any time, next time, the first time, the last time，hardly/scarcely…when, no sooner…than
地点状语从句	where, wherever，everywhere
条件状语从句	if, so/as long as, unless, on condition that, in case, supposing（that）, providing/provided（that）
原因状语从句	because, since, as, for in that, now that, not that…but that…
目的状语从句	so that, in order that,lest, for fear that, in case
结果状语从句	so that, so/such…that
方式状语从句	as,（just）as…so…,as if/though, like, the way
让步状语从句	though/although, as, while, even if/though, whatever, whichever, whenever, wherever, whoever, however, whether…or not, no matter how/what/when/where
比较状语从句	than, as…as, not as/so…as, the+ 比较级 …，the+ 比较级 …

二、状语从句的用法

（一）时间状语从句

1. when,while, as 的用法

（1）when，"当……时候"，引导时间状语从句，表示主句的动作和从句的动作同时或先后发生。when 引导的时间状语从句中的动词可以用延续性动词，也可以用终止性动词。

I feel very happy when you come to see me.

When you are crossing the street, you must be careful.

I worked for a foreign company when I was in Shanghai.

（2）while，"与……同时，在……期间"，引导的从句常用延续性动词或表示状态的动词。

They rushed in while we were discussing problems.

（3）as，"正当……，一边……一边，随着"。

Helen heard the story as she washed clothes.

2. before, after 的用法

（1）before 和 after 表示的是主句和从句动作发生的前后关系。before 引导的从句动作通常发生在主句动作之后；after 引导的从句动作通常发生在主句动作之前。

They had got everything ready before I arrived.

We'll arrive after you have left.

I arrived after he（had）left.

（2）after 引导时间状语从句时，前面可以有副词修饰。

She started the job soon after she left the university.

Peter took to drink shortly after he lost his job.

（3）before 引导时间状语从句可以用在"It will be + 一段时间 +before…"或"It wasn't/won't be long before…"句型中。

It will be a long time before we meet again.

It won't be long before you get used to wearing glasses.

（4）before, after 引导的时间状语从句的主语和主句主语相同时，从句也可改写为 before/after+doing 形式。

They had dinner before going to the concert.

I made my decision after talking to my father.

3. until, till 的用法

"直到……"，表示一个动作持续到另一个时刻或某一个动作发生，until 只能用于句首。肯定句中用延续性动词，否定句中用非延续性动词。

I will wait until/till she comes back.

Until they had finished the work, they did not go home.

He didn't go to bed until he finished his homework.

4. as soon as, the moment/minute/instant, immediately, directly 等的用法

这些词或短语引导的时间状语从句中的动作与主句中的动作几乎同时发生。

I will write to you as soon as I arrive there.

We'll set off the moment/ minute/instant you are ready.

Immediately/Directly she got the letter, she went to see him.

5. since 的用法

（1）since 引导的从句中一般用非延续性动词，时态为一般过去时，主句用完成时态。

Since he graduated, he has worked in the city.

We haven't seen each other since we left school.

（2）since 引导的从句中如果用延续性动词或状态动词，所表示的就是动作或状态的完成或结束。

Since he was ill（=Since he was all right），I haven't heard from him.

It has been three years since he lived here（=since he left here）.

（3）since 可以用作介词，后接点时刻。since 还可以用作副词，可与 ever 连用。

I have lived here since 1990.

He has been writing the book since five years ago.

He left home last year and we haven't seen him（ever）since.

She moved to London last May and has since worked there.

6. hardly/scarcely…when, no sooner…than 的用法

在 hardly/scarcely…when, no sooner…than 句型中，主句要用过去完成时，从句要用一般过去时。该句型置于句首时，要使用部分倒装。

I had hardly/scarcely entered the room when it began to rain.

No sooner had we sat down than the telephone rang.

7. every time, any time, next time, the first time, the last time 等的用法

这些短语有时可以引导时间状语从句。

Every time I catch a cold, my nose runs.

Next time you come here, don't forget to bring me the book.

（二）地点状语从句

常见引导地点状语从句的连词有 where, wherever, anywhere, everywhere 等。

You have right to live where you want.

The school will be built where there used to be a church.

I always think of you everywhere we stayed together.

（三）条件状语从句

If（如果，假若），so/as long as（只要），unless（除非、如果不），on condition that（条件是、在……条件下），in case（如果，假使），supposing（that）（假设、假定），providing/provided（that）（如果、假如、在……条件下）

I'll visit the Great Wall if it doesn't rain tomorrow.

I won't leave the hospital unless the doctors tells me she's all right.

I will agree to come on condition that she is invited too.

We'll start working immediately as/so long as you accept our condition.

> in case

in case 意为"以防、以防万一"时，引导目的状语从句，多用陈述语气，也可用虚拟语气，此时从句谓语动词用"should+ 动词原形"的形式；意为"如果、假使"时，引导条件状语从句。

试比较：Take an umbrella with you, in case it rains/should rain.（目的）

In case John comes, Please tell him to wait.（条件）

（四）原因状语从句

because（因为），since（既然），as（因为、由于），for（由于、因为），in that（原因是、因为），now that（既然、由于），not that...but that...（不是……而是……）

Because it was raining outside, I didn't go to visit him.

Since you say so, I suppose it is true.

She didn't hear us come in as she was asleep.

> because/since/for

① because 表示因果关系的语气最强，用来回答 why 的问句，所引出的原因往往是听话人所不知道或最感兴趣的，because 引导的原因状语从句往往比主句显得更重要。

I'm leaving because I am fed up with the boss.

② since 引出的原因往往是人们已知的事实，因此经常译成"既然……"，通常放在句首。since 引导的从句是次要的，重点强调主句的内容。

Since Monday is Bob's birthday, let's give him a party.

③ as 与 since 用法差不多，所引出的理由在听话人看来已经很明显，或已为听话人所熟悉而不需要用 because 加强。as 引导的从句与主句具有同等的重要性。

As the weather was very fine, we decided to climb a mountain.

（五）目的状语从句

so that（为了，以便），in order that（为了、以便、目的在于），lest（唯恐、免得、以免），for fear that（唯恐、以免），in case（以防万一、以防）。

He emphasized this point again and again, lest/for fear that she should forget.

Tom works hard so that/in order that he could make much money.

（六）结果状语从句

so that（因此、所以），so/such…that（如此……以至于……）

He spoke very clearly, so that everyone understood him.

It was such terrible weather that we couldn't finish building on time.

> so that

既可以引导目的状语从句，又可以引导结果状语从句，区别如下：

①引导目的状语从句时表示一种可能性或目的，引导结果状语从句时表示一种事实。

② so that 引导的目的状语从句中常含有 can, could, may, might, would 等情态动词，而 so that 引导的结果状语从句中一般没有情态动词。

③ so that 引导的目的状语从句与主句之间一般不用逗号隔开，而 so that 引导的结果状语从句与主句之间可以用逗号隔开。

She left early so that she could catch the train.（目的）

She left early, so that she caught the train.（结果）

（七）方式状语从句

As（按照，照……方式），(just) as…so…（正如……一样，……也……），as if/though（好像），like（像……，如同），the way（像……那样，以……方式）。

Just as the French enjoy wine, so the British enjoy beer.

Mary didn't see things the way her mother did.

Michael said nothing, but simply nodded, as if/though he completely understood.

（八）让步状语从句

though/although（虽然、尽管），as（虽然、尽管），while（虽然、尽管），even if/though（即使、尽管），whatever（无论什么、不管什么），whichever（不论哪个），whenever（无论何时），wherever（无论哪里），whoever（无论谁），however（无论如何、不管怎样），whether…or not（不管是否），no matter how/what/when/where（不管怎样/什么/何时/何处）。

Although they are cheap, they never go out of style.

We will take a trip even if/though the weather is bad.

Whichever route you choose, it will take three hours to get there.

Whoever you are, you must obey the regulations.

No matter what happens, he will not say a word.

as 引导让步状语从句时，从句须倒装，即将表语、状语或谓语部分的实义动词提到句首；如果表语是名词，应省略冠词。though 引导让步状语从句时，从句可以倒装，也可以不倒装。although 引导让步状语从句时，从句不能倒装。though/although 不能和 but 连用，但可以跟 yet, still 连用。

Although/Though the machine is old, it is still in perfect order.

= Old as/though the machine is, it is still in perfect order.

（九）比较状语从句

than（比），as...as（像……一样……），not as/so...as（不像……一样……），the + 比较级 ...，the + 比较级 ...（越……，就越……）。

She dances as gracefully as her younger sister.

The more difficult the questions are, the less likely he is able to answer them.

> than/as...as...

①在 than 和 as...as... 引导比较状语从句中，常省略和主句相同的部分，只留下相比较的部分。

Billy is much taller than his friend（is）.

②在 than 和 as...as... 引导比较状语从句中，常用助动词的某种形式或情态动词代替与主句相同的谓语部分。

Jack works as hard as Jim does.

He loves me more than you do.

专项练习题

1. The children were enjoying their dinner ____ a stranger knocked at the door.

    A. then   B. while

    C. as   D. when

2. The roof fell ____ he had time to dash into the room to save his baby.

    A. as   B. before

    C. after   D. until

3. Don't be afraid of asking for information ____ it is needed.

    A. when   B. after

    C. although   D. unless

4. Nearly a week passed ____ the girl was able to explain what has happened to her.

    A. while   B. till

    C. that   D. before

5. He was about to go to bed ____ the doorbell rang.

    A. while   B. as

    C. before   D. since

6. Mr. Brown has worked in our school ____ he came in 2020.

    A. when   B. whether

    C. before   D. since

7. They will have a picnic in the park ____ it's a fine day tomorrow.

    A. if   B. as if

    C. unless   D. although

8. Mary got up so late ____ she had to go to work without breakfast.

    A. as   B. that

    C. when   D. for

9. I gave up this video game, ____ I didn't have enough money.

    A. though   B. because

    C. unless   D. even if

10. You'd better take the map with you ____ you can't get lost.

    A. after   B. as soon as

    C. though   D. so that

11. I didn't realize he was a famous writer ____ you told me.

    A. until   B. when

    C. although   D. if

12. I didn't know the answer to the question ____ my classmate told me.

    A. until   B. after

    C. as soon as   D. if

13. Hearing the news, she was so sad ____ I has to stay here.

    A. what   B. as

    C. that   D. but

14. Unhealthy ____ he was, he persisted in doing the dangerous experiment.

    A. although   B. unless

    C. as   D. in case

15. It is known to all that ＿＿ you exercise regularly, you will be able to keep a good figure.

      A. because   B. if

      C. unless   D. even though

16. ＿＿ dictionary you want to buy, I will be willing to pay for it.

      A. Wherever   B. Whenever

      C. However   D. Whichever

17. Scarcely had they left ＿＿ soldiers armed with guns arrived.

      A. before   B. than

      C. while   D. when

18. ＿＿ I am willing to help, I don't have much time available.

      A. When   B. As

      C. While   D. On condition that

19. I was so familiar with him that I recognized his voice ＿＿ I picked up the phone.

      A. while   B. after

      C. lest   D. the minute

20. People can always manage to do more things, no matter ＿＿ full their schedule is.

      A. how   B. what

      C. when   D. where

21. We have no right to accuse him ＿＿ there is enough evidence to prove that he cheated in the exam.

      A. as though   B. as soon as

      C. in case   D. unless

22. I've earned my own living ＿＿ I was seventeen, doing all kinds of jobs.

      A. since   B. now that

      C. although   D. if

23. English is a course to learn in the university, ＿＿ students' majors are.

      A. whatever   B. even if

      C. however   D. no matter

24. I didn't need to send the book to Tom, ＿＿ I'll see him tomorrow.

      A. though   B. unless

      C. for   D. when

25. No sooner had he finished his speech, ____ the students started cheering.

    A. since   B. as

    C. when   D. than

26. Everyday is full of happiness ____ we are thankful for what we have.

    A. as soon as   B. as long as

    C. so as to   D. immediately

27. He suddenly woke up, ____ he had heard someone call his name loudly.

    A. lest   B. as if

    C. even if   D. so that

28. It was the middle of the night ____ my roommate woke me up and asked me to play a game with him.

    A. that   B. what

    C. which   D. when

29. Please call my secretary to arrange a meeting this afternoon, ____ it is convenient for you.

    A. whenever   B. however

    C. whichever   D. wherever

30. The elder still prefer the traditional way, ____ the online booking system is more convenient.

    A. as if   B. unless

    C. though   D. if

31. ____ you are free today, why not play football with me?

    A. Since   B. Because

    C. For   D. If

32. I won't go with you ____ I am busy doing my homework now.

    A. for   B. because

    C. so   D. since

33. ____ was fine, I went out for a walk.

    A. For it   B. As it

    C. As there   D. Because of

34. He came here not because he needed money ____ he needed your support.

    A. but also   B. but

    C. but because   D. not because

35. Michael got up early ＿＿＿ he would not be late for the plane.

　A. so that　　　　　　　　B. in order to

　C. to　　　　　　　　　　D. such that

第五节　主谓一致

一、何为"主谓一致"？

　　主谓一致是指主语和谓语两个语法成分之间保持一致。在英语中，主谓一致主要是指用作主语的名词、代词和用作谓语的动词在人称、数等方面保持一致。

二、主谓一致应遵循的原则

（一）语法一致原则：谓语动词数的形式取决于主语的单（复）数形式

　（1）单数名词／代词、不可数名词作主语时，谓语动词用单数形式。

The girl's idea about the problem is very novel and interesting.

The traffic has been a problem for a long time.

That sounds good, but could you give some specific reasons?

　（2）有些单数集体名词是不可数名词，如：clothing, machinery, furniture, equipment, baggage 等。

The furniture is made of wood and should be kept away from fire.

This equipment has saved the lives of a large number of patients.

　（3）"many a+ 单数名词"作主语时，谓语动词用单数形式。

Many a student likes to take Professor Li's class.

　（4）"more than one+ 单数名词"虽然在意义上有复数概念，但作主语时，谓语动词常用单数形式。"more+ 复数名词 +than one"作主语时，谓语动词则用复数形式。

More than one person is involved in this case.

More visitors than one have complained about the service here.

　（5）"a（n）+ 单数名词 + or two"作主语时，谓语动词用单数形式。但"one or two+ 复数名词"作主语时，谓语动词则用复数形式。

A student or two has failed the exam.

One or two students have failed the exam.

（6）常用作复数或只有复数形式的名词作主语时，谓语动词用复数形式。如：clothes, belongings（财物），earnings（薪水，收入），savings（积蓄，存款），surroundings（环境），odds（可能性），remains（剩余物，残留物），goods（尚品），fireworks（烟花表演），thanks（感谢）等。

The clothes are not suitable for everyday wear.

（7）表示双数意义的复数名词作主语时，谓语动词常用复数形式。如：glasses, sunglasses, scissors（剪刀），shoes, socks, gloves, trousers, jeans, shorts, spectacles（眼镜）等。

His glasses were broken by his danghter last night.

（8）由 and 或 both…and… 连接连个并列主语时，谓语动词多用复数形式。但如果并列主语指的是一个人、物、概念或不可分割的整体时，谓语动词要用单数形式。如：bread and butter（涂黄油的面包），a watch and chain（一块带链的表），law and order（社会秩序），a knife and fork（一副刀叉）等。

Peter and Billy compete with each other for the contract.

War and peace is a constant theme in history.

A teacher and writer is going to give us a speech this evening.

（9）当 and 连接的单数名词由 each, every, no 等修饰时，谓语动词用单数形式。

Each book and（each）magazine has to be returned on time.

No teacher and（no）student likes this textbook.

（10）"to to，doing，疑问词/whether+to do" 作主语时，谓语动词常用单数形式。and 连接两个并列的上述结构时，如表示单一概念，谓语动词用单数形式；如表示两个不同的概念，则谓语动词用复数形式。

To do this job well means a lot of effort.

Whether she is coming or not doesn't matter too much.

Reading and writing are very important during the primary school.

（11）"分数/百分数 + of + 名词/代词" 作主语时，谓语动词要与 of 后面的名词或代词的数保持一致。

Two thirds of the food has been sent to the area.

80% of the students in our school are girls.

（12）"a number of+ 复数名词/代词" 作主语时，谓语动词用复数形式；"the number of + 复数名词/代词" 作主语时，谓语动词用单数形式。

A number of children are playing in the park.

The number of clients of this company is rather small.

（13）"a quantity of/a lot of/lots of/plenty of + 不可数名词或可数名词复数" 作主语时，谓语动词要与名词的数保持一致。但 "quantities of + 不可数名词/可数名词复数" 作主语时，谓语动词要用复数形式。

A vast quantity of beer was sold yesterday.

A large quantity of books were found in his room.

Great quantities of sand were washed down the hillside by rain.

（14）"a great（good）deal of/ a large amount of/ a bit of + 不可数名词"作主语时，谓语动词用单数形式。但 "large/increasing/small amounts of + 不可数名词"作主语时，谓语动词用复数形式。

A good deal of money has been spent on this project.

A large amount of electricity was wasted last month.

Large amount of time have been invested in the experiment.

（15）"分类词 + of + 名词"作主语时，谓语动词要与分类词的单、复数保持一致。常用的分类词包括：kind, sort, form, piece, series, portion, species, type 等。

This kind of competition is not what we want.

All kinds of flowers blossom in Spring.

（16）在倒装句中，谓语动词的形式要与其后的主语保持一致。

Under these books is a notebook where she has written a lot of her experiences.

Here are the pictures you have been looking forward to.

（二）意义一致原则：谓语动词数的形式取决于主语的单（复）数意义

（1）单数名词作主语时，从语法形式上讲，谓语动词一般要用单数形式。但有时作主语的单数名词表示复数含义，此时谓语动词要用复数形式，达到意义一致。

集体名词，如：army, class, committee, company, crowd, couple, group, party, population, team, public, family, faculty, audience, staff 等作主语时，谓语动词的形式取决于主语的意义。当主语表示整体概念时，谓语动词用单数；当主语表示集体中的个体成员时，谓语动词用复数。

有生命的集体名词，如：youth, police, people, personnel, cattle, folk 等作主语时，谓语动词通常用复数形式。

The police are looking into the accident.

（2）有些名词虽然是复数形式，但意义上表示单数，作主语时谓语动词用单数形式。

The bad new is that only 13% of the people got the salary.

（3）表示"时间、距离、金钱、重量"等的复数名词作主语时，如表示整体概念，谓语动词用单数形式。

Ten years is just a moment in history.

Forty miles is too long a way to walk in a day.

（4）以 –ics 结尾表示学科等的名词作主语时，谓语动词一般用单数。如：physics, economics, electronics, mathematics, ethics, politics statistics, gymnastics, athletics 等。

当 economics, electronics, ethics, politics statistics 表示其他含义时，可当复数用，作主语时谓语动词用复数形式。

Pyhsics is one of the hardest subjects for a middle school student.

Statistics is a basic course at the business school.

（5）"a/this/that pair/suit of + 复数名词"作主语时，谓语动词用单数形式。

That pair of shoes has already been sold.

（6）"the + 形容词 / 分词"表示一类人或事物，作主语时多表示复数含义，谓语动词常用复数形式。当表示个体、不可数事物或抽象概念时，谓语动词用单数。

According to the research, the unemployed tend to be out of work for a long time.

The injured in the accident is a friend of mine.

（7）在"one of + 复数名词 + 定语从句"结构中，从句一般修饰复数名词，因此从句的谓语动词要用复数形式。当 one of 前面有 the only, the very, the mere 等修饰时，从句一般是修饰单数名词的，此时从句的谓语动词要用单数形式。

Jack is one of the journalists who were awarded a prize at that time.

Jack is the only one of the journalists who was awarded a prize at that time.

（8）由 as well as, as much as, along with, together with, with, including, followed by, in addition to, like, unlike, except, but, besides, no less than, rather than, accompanied by, instead of, more than 等连接的并列主语在意义上更强调前面的主语，谓语动词通常与前面主语的人称和数保持一致。

The girl, together with her classmates, has gone to plant trees.

The teacher, with all his students, is going to have a picnic this weekend.

（三）就近一致原则：谓语动词数的形式取决于最靠近它的词的单（复）数形式

（1）"名词 / 代词 + or + 名词 / 代词"作主语时，谓语动词的单复数取决于 or 后面的词。

You or Mary is to be sent to solve the problem.

（2）either…or…, neither…nor…, not only…but also… 连接的名词或代词作主语时，谓语动词要与后面的词保持一致。

Neither the father nor the children know anything about the matter.

Either you or Jack is going to meet them at the station.

Not only the students but also the teacher enjoys listening to music.

（3）在 There be 句型中，谓语动词的单复数形式取决于离其近的主语。

There is two knives, a pen and some books on the desk.

There is a teacher, and some parents at the school gate.

专项练习题

1. Not only I but also Mike ____ to attend the meeting.

    A. were allowed   B. was allowed

    C. am allowed   D. allows

2. Electronics ____ a new subject of this university, so it is not so well developed as other subjects.

    A. were   B. was

    C. is   D. are

3. Every possible means ____ to prevent air pollution, but it doesn't work.

    A. use   B. are used

    C. has been used   D. have been used

4. Amy, together with her brothers, ____ a warm welcome when returning to the village last week.

    A. is given   B. are given

    C. was given   D. were given

5. As is mentioned above, the number of the students in high school____.

    A. is increasing   B. are increasing

    C. increase   D. have increased

6. Martin is one of the students that ____ a good command of public speaking skills in his class.

    A. had   B. have

    C. has   D. have had

7. Ten thousand dollars ____ a lot of money for the family in the remote village.

    A. are   B. is

    C. were   D. be

8. The United Nations ____ trying to find a better way to bring the two sides together now.

    A. is   B. are

    C. were   D. was

9. The government ____ decided to reduce military expenditure.

    A. are   B. is

    C. has   D. have

10. My best friend and adviser _____ mind again.

    A. have changed   B. has changed his

    C. have changed their   D. has change his

11. Many a father _____ more time with his children when they were young.

    A. have regretted not spending   B. has regretted not to spend

    C. has regretted not spending   D. has regretted spending not

12. The committee _____ among themselves for four hours.

    A. has been arguing   B. have been arguing

    C. have been argued   D. has been argued

13. There _____ in this room.

    A. are too many rooms   B. are too much room

    C. are plenty of rooms   D. is plenty of room

14. None of your advice _____ acceptable.

    A. are   B. is

    C. listens   D. sound

15. Three–fourths of the surface of the earth _____ sea.

    A. are covering   B. is covering with

    C. covers with   D. is covered with

16. No noise and no smoking _____ allowed here.

    A. are   B. is

    C. have   D. has

17. The volunteers try to convince people of the fact that many species _____ in danger of dying out.

    A. are   B. is

    C. was   D. were

18. He is the only one of the boys who _____ never late for school in his class.

    A. are   B. is

    C. have been   D. were

19. The singer and dancer _____ going to give us a performance tonight.

    A. are   B. is

    C. were   D. has

20. Your trousers _____ too old. A pair of new trousers _____ necessary for you.

    A. is, is   B. are, is

    C. are, are   D. is, are

21. Jane, rather than her brother, _____ live coverage of the football match on the Internet now.

A. was watching
B. are watching
C. is watching
D. were watching

22. All the employees except the manager _____ to work online at home.

A. encourages
B. encourage
C. is encouraged
D. are encouraged

23. A large percentage of the work _____ done yesterday.

A. have been
B. has been
C. were
D. was

24. This kind of problems _____ to deal with.

A. have difficulty
B. has difficulty
C. are difficult
D. is difficult

25. All sorts of furniture _____ display in the shop.

A. are in
B. is in
C. are on
D. is on

26. Writing stories and articles _____ what I enjoy most.

A. is
B. are
C. was
D. was

27. Both the secretary and the manager _____ agreed to attend the meeting.

A. has
B. have
C. are
D. was

28. Where to get the materials and how to get them _____ at the meeting.

A. have not discussed
B. have not been discussed
C. has not discussed
D. was not discussed

29. Large quantities of water _____ needed for the purpose of cooling.

A. is
B. are
C. has
D. have

30. The survey shows that doing three hours' outdoor exercise a week _____ good for one's health.

A. are
B. is
C. was
D. were

第六节 特殊句式

一、强调句

强调是指在英语句子中，通过一定的语法手段来加强某些成分。强调的方法通常有词汇强调和语法强调两种。

（一）词汇强调

1. do 表示强调

肯定的祈使句、一般现在时或一般过去时的肯定句中可以用 do 的适当形式强调动词，意为"务必、一定"或"确实"。

Do come early.

She did come last week.

I do believe that you can succeed.

He does know how to do that.

2. only, even, alone, just, ever, very, too, at all, on earth, in the world, rather, entirely, completely, if ever, if any 等表示强调

You are the only person here that can speak English.

How on earth can she afford that?

He is the very man you're looking for.

3. however, whatever, wherever, whenever, whoever, whichever, no matter how/ what/where/when/ who/which 等表示强调

However/No matter how hard he tried, he couldn't lift the box.

Whoever/No matter who you are, you should obey the rule.

（二）语法强调

1. It is/was + 被强调部分 + that/who + 其他

该句式是强调句型的基本结构。被强调的部分通常为主语、宾语或状语。被强调部分如果是人，其后可以用 who 或 that 均可；被强调的部分如果是物，则只能用 that 连接。

It was Mary that/who gave away the secret.（强调主语）

It was Mr. Grant that we invited to give us a lecture.（强调宾语）

It is only when one is ill that one knows the value of health.（强调状语）

It was not until you pointed it out to me that I realized my mistake.（强调状语）

2. "what…is/was…"结构可用来强调主语从句中表物的主语或宾语

What I need is your support.

What matters is quality.

What is really important is we can get there on time.

3. 一般疑问句的强调句式是 Is/Was it + 被强调部分 + that / who... 特殊疑问句的强调句式是 "特殊疑问词 +is / was+（that）+ 句子"。特殊疑问句中只有疑问词可以被强调

Was it Sally that/who phoned just now?

How is it（that）your answer differs from others?

What is it（that）you want me to say?

二、倒装句

分类	特征	例句
完全倒装	将全部谓语置于主语之前	There stood a desk against the wall.
部分倒装	将谓语动词中的助动词、be 动词或情态动态提至主语之前，而谓语的主体部分留在主语之后	Only in this way can you lose weight.

（一）完全倒装

1. there be/like/live/exist/seem/appear/come/lie/happen 等句型为全部倒装

There seems to be no reason for changing our plan.

There exists some misunderstanding between them.

2. 如句首是表示时间、地点、方位的副词（here, there, now, then，down,up, in, out, off, back, away 等），谓语动词为 be, go, come, exist, fall, follow, lie, remain, seem, stand 等动词，且句子主语为名词，用全部倒装。如果主语为代词，则不需要倒装

Here comes the bus.

There comes the man about whom we have just talked.

Now is the hour when I say goodbye.

The door opened and in came the teacher.

3. 以作地点状语的介词短语开头，句子全部倒装。主语为代词时，不倒装

At the top of the hill stands an old temple.

By his side sat the faithful pet dog.

It stands at the top of the hill.

4. 系表结构中，主语较长时，为使句子平衡，用全部倒装

Gone are the day when China had to depend on foreign oil.

Among the students was the respectable professor.

（二）部分倒装

1. 以 so, neither, nor 开头的句子，重复前面句子的内容，要用部分倒装

（1）neither/nor 用于否定句，"neither/nor+ 助动词（情态动词）+ 主语"结构表示"也不……"；so 用于肯定句，"so + 助动词（情态动词）+ 主语"结构表示"也……"。

I haven't been to the Great Wall. Neither/Nor has he.

She speaks English fluently, so does he.

（2）当两个句子的主语一致时，so 引导的句子不倒装，表示"确认"。

He has succeeded in doing the experiment. So he has.

She passed the difficult test of English. So she did.

2. 以表示否定或部分否定意义的词或短语开头，句子用部分倒装

（1）否定词：never, seldom, rarely, little, hardly, scarcely, not often, nowhere。

Rarely/ Seldom does he go to the movies.

Never before have I seen such a good film.

Little did he realize how important the meeting was.

Not until recently did I find out my mistake.

（2）介词短语：at no time（从来没有），by no means（决不），in no way（决不），in no case（决不），on no account（决不），in/under no circumstances（决不）。

Under no circumstance should you lend him any money.

On no account must you accept his invitation.

At no time will China first use nuclear weapons.

（3）连词：neither…nor, not…until, no sooner…than, hardly…when, not only…but also。

Not only did he hear it, but he saw it as well.

Hardly had he come back when it began to snow.

Neither does she know nor care what happened.

3. 以 well, often, long 等方式状语或频度状语开头，句子用部分倒装

Well do I remember the day I saw her the first time.

Often did he visit me in the past.

Long did we wait before we heard the news.

Many a time has Mike given me help.

4. 以"only+ 状语"结构开头，句子用部分倒装

Only in this way can you learn English well.

Only when she came home did she learn the news.

5. 当 so/such…that… 结构中的 so 或 such 连同其所修饰的成分位于句首时，主句要

用部分倒装

So carelessly did he drive that he almost ran his car into a tree.

To such an extent did his health deteriorate that he was forced to retire.

6. if 引导的虚拟条件句，如果句中有 had, should, were，常可以省略 if，从句使用部分倒装

Had he had time, he would have come to help you.

Should it rain tomorrow, we would cancel the meeting.

Were you to come next week, you would see him.

（三）其他倒装形式

（1）as, though 引导的让步状语从句中，表语或状语要置于句首，形成倒装。当名词置于句首时，前面不加任何冠词。

Child as/though he is, he knows a lot of things about the solar system.

Fail as/though I did, I would never give up.

（2）比较状语从句和方式状语从句中，do, be 可以放在主语之前，形成倒装。"the + 比较级……，the + 比较级……"结构中，状语、表语或宾语要置于句首，形成倒装。

He traveled a great deal, as did most of his friends.

Harry is unusually tall, as are his brothers.

City dwellers have a higher death rate than do country people.

The harder you work, the happier you feel.

三、省略句

一个句子的一个或多个成分有时会被省略掉，但句子意义仍然完整，这样的句子叫作省略句。

（I）Hope you to come back early.

（Is there）anything important?

Have you finished the work? —Not yet.

Will you join us? —I should love to（join you）.

He won't go to the party. —Why not（go to the party）?

The meeting lasted（for）three hours.

You will never succeed（in）that way.

He didn't come back until（it was）very late.

有些情况下，当省略了某个词、某个短语或某个句子时，还要用某个词代替省略的成分。常用的代替词有 do, so, not, to, neither, nor, do so, do that, do it, one（s）, the same 等。

1. do 的用法

比较状语从句、方式状语从句或简略回答中，do 可以代替"谓语 + 宾语（状语）"。

He speaks English better than you do.

You will get there as soon as they do.

She cooks omelets in butter as they do in France.

Did you see the film? —Yes, I did.

2. so, not 的用法

（1）肯定句中，so 可以代替词、短语或句子，作 expect, hope, imagine, suppose, think, believe, fear, guess, be afraid 等的宾语，还可以用于 It seems/appears… 结构中。

Has he finished his job? — I hope so.

She was not angry at first, but became so after a while.

He is my best friend and I hope he will always remain so.

（2）not 代替否定的句子，用法与 so 相似。在与 believe, expect, imagine, suppose, think 等连用时，也可以用 not…so。

He will return at the weekend. — I am afraid not.

Are they reliable? — It seems/appears not.

Is he coming? —I expect not.（ =I don't expect so. ）

3. to 的用法

to 代替不定式，常用在 refuse, want, seem, intend, mean, expect, hope, like, be afraid, prefer, care, forget, wish, try 等动词之后。

I asked him to see the film, but he didn't want to（ see the film ）.

I suggest that she reconsider it, but she refused to（ reconsider it ）.

Will you stay for lunch? —I hope to（ stay for lunch ）.

4. do so, do that, do it 的用法

do so 代替"谓语 + 宾语（状语）"结构。"谓语 + 宾语"结构中，so 可代替 it 或 that。

She said she would go with me, but she didn't do so.

They played chess after supper and I watched them do so/that/it.

5. one, that 的用法

（1）one 可以代替单数可数名词，复数形式为 ones，代指人或物；that 既可以代替单数可数名词也可以代替不可数名词，只能代指物。

I forgot to bring a pen. Can you lend me one?

I prefer red roses to white ones.

The novel is as interesting as the one/that I read last year.

The population of Tokyo is larger than that of London.

（2）one 可以有前置定语或后置定语，that 只有后置定语。

The officer is the one who gives orders.

Those shoes are too small. We must buy some new ones.

Your answer to the question is better than that of Mary.

（3）不加定冠词，one 表示泛指；that 表示特指。

The music is as sweet as that we heard yesterday.

A poem in English is usually harder to understand than one in Chinese.

6. the same 的用法

the same 一般指物，可以代替名词短语、从句、形容词短语或比较结构等。

Tom ordered two glasses of beer. I ordered the same.

We can trust Jane. I think I could say the same of her husband.

These apples are just as sweet as the ones we had last week. They taste the same.

四、There be 句型（某地有某物）

There be 句型为倒装句，谓语动词的单复数遵循就近原则，be 动词根据离它最近的名词决定。

There is some water in the glass.

There are two glasses of juice on the table.

1. There be+ 可数 n.+ 地点状语

There is a box in/under/behind/next to/near/ by/ in front of/between the two desks.

There are some apples on the tree.

There aren't any apples on the tree.（= There are no apples on the tree）

就主语进行提问：There is a box on the desk.　→　What's on the desk?

※ 当主语是"物"时，用 What is...? 当主语是"人"时，用 Who is...?

就主语的数量进行提问：How many boxes are there on the desk?

2. There be + 不可数 n.+ 地点状语

There is some milk in the glass.

Is there any milk in the glass?

There ins't any milk in the glass（=There is no milk in the glass）.

就主语（不可数）前面的"量"进行提问：How much milk is there in the glass?

3. There be + 主语 + doing sth. + 地点状语

There is a bird singing in the tree.

4. There + 情态动词 + be

There used to be a school in that area.

There may have been an accident.

5. There+ 动词

There + live/exist/remain/lie/stand/belong/appear/seem/happen 等，用来表示状态。

There seems to be no reason for changing our plan.

Do you think there remains nothing to be done?

6. There be+ 形容词

There be + likely/certain/sure/going/bound 等，表示可能性。

There is going to be a heavy snow.

There is sure to be some rain tonight.

7. There is no point/use（in）+ 动名词

"……是没有意义的，……是无用的"

There is no point（in）making the same suggestions.

There is no use（in）trying to dissuade him.

专项练习题

1. It was for this reason ____ his uncle moved from Chicago and lost touch with his children.

    A. which   B. why

    C. that   D. how

2. No sooner ____to school than ____ to clean the classroom.

    A. she had got, did she begin   B. had she got, she began

    C. she got, she began   D. did she get, she had begun

3. Only by practicing a few hours every day ____ the skill in playing the violin.

    A. you can master   B. can you master

    C. you will master   D. did you master

4. It was not until 1992 ____ baseball became an official event of the Olympic Games.

    A. then   B.which

    C. that   D. when

5. ____ that this region was so rich in natural resources.

    A. Little he knew   B. Little did he know

    C. Little he did know   D. Little he had known

6. Not until I shouted at the top of my voice ____ his head.

    A. had he turned   B. did he turn

    C. he didn't turn   D. he had turned

7. Under no circumstances ____ to hand in his invention to the authorities.

    A. would he agree   B. he agreed

    C. should not be agree   D. did he agreed

8. She said she would go and she ____ go.

    A. didn't   B. did

    C. would   D. will

9. In a chemical change, energy cannot be created, ____.

    A. nor can it be destroyed   B. not can it be destroyed

    C. so can it not be destroyed   D. either it cannot be destroyed

10. ____ that some foreign guests will come to our college tomorrow.

    A. The news here comes   B. Here comes the news

    C. Here come the news   D. The news come here

11. ____ do we go for picnics.

    A. Certainly   B. Seldom

    C. Sometimes   D. once

12. Little ____ we think his speech had made so deep an impression on his audience.

    A. have   B. had

    C. did   D. should

13. So badly ____ that he had to go to the hospital.

    A. he injured   B. was he injured

    C. he was injured   D. did he injure

14. ____ she would one day become Miss Hong Kong.

    A. I realize little   B. I did little realize

    C. Little did I realize   D. Little I realized

15. ____ had David reached school when the bell rang.

    A. No sooner   B. Although

    C. Only   D. Hardly

16. By no means ____ look down upon the poor.

    A. we shall   B. we should

    C. ought we   D. should we

17. ____, Tom knows what is right and what is wrong.

    A. Child as he is   B. A child as he

    C. A child as he is   D. As he is a child

18. Not only____ be interesting to us, but also its English will help us in composition.

    A. the novel will   B. will the novel

    C. is the novel   D. the novel is

19.. ____, you won't be able to do it alone.

    A. However you try hard   B. You try hard however

    C. However hard you try   D. Hard you try however

20. So excited ____ that he didn't notice a big stone on the ground.

    A. he seemed   B. did he seem

    C. was he seeming   D. he did seem

第三章　语法的综合运用

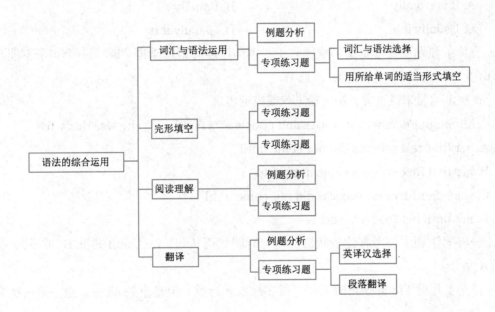

 第一节　词汇与语法运用

一、例题分析

1. ____ kinds of decorative art: handicrafts and fine arts.

    A. There is two   B. There are two

    C. In two   D. Two

【分析】该题主要考查语法知识主谓一致中的"there be"句型，kinds 复数形式，故选 B。

【译文】有两种装饰艺术：手工艺术和美术。

2. He taught school for many years and became a doctor in 1975____of forty.

    A. age   B. the age

    C. at the age   D. he was at the age

【分析】该题主要考查介词短语，在某人多少岁固定用法：at the age of... 故选 C。

【译文】他教书很多年了，1975 年在他 40 岁的时候他成为一名医生。

3. ____, incense is made in powder form or in stacks.

    A. It is usually   B. Usually

    C. Usually it is   D. Usually it is

【分析】该题主要考查副词修饰句子。本句已经有谓语动词"is"，一个句子不能存在两个谓语，所以排除 A、C、D，故选 B。

【译文】通常来说，香会制成粉末状或成堆出现。

4. Although Fiona wrote stories and poems as a child, ____she was thirty five.

A. her first real success did not come until

B. her real first success came until not

C. since her first real success did not come until

D. not until her first real success

【分析】该题主要考查让步状语从句与时间状语从句，no...until 排除 B，再根据句意，故选 A。

【译文】尽管 Fiona 孩童时期写了很多故事和诗歌，但是直到 35 岁，她才第一次真正成功。

5. A line segment, which is part of a straight line, begins at one point ____at another.

    A. ending   B. by ending

    C. the end is   D. and ends

【分析】该题主要考查 and 的并列用法，横线前后形式一致，故选 D。

【译文】线段是直线的一部分，从一个点开始到另一个点结束。

6. An air brake is____the power of compressed air to stop a wheel from turning.

    A. a brake that uses   B. a brake used to

    C. what any brake is used for   D. that brake is used for

【分析】该题主要考查定语从句，that 充当从句主语，横线后句子完整，故选 A。

【译文】空气刹车是使用压缩空气的力量来阻挡车轮旋转的刹车。

7. Steam turbines weigh____that produce the same amount of power.

　　A. less than piston engines and　　　B. less than piston engines

　　C. piston engines are less than　　　D. in piston engines less than

【分析】该题主要考查比较级及五大基本句型之一，根据句意表示前者比后者轻，故选 B。

【译文】蒸汽轮机的重量比产生相同功率的活塞发动机轻。

8. ____one-celled organisms, nearly all animals have a nervous system of some kind.

　　A. Some　　　　　　　　　　B. The

　　C. Except for　　　　　　　　D. Despite

【分析】该题主要考查状语从句，except for 表排除，故选 C。

【译文】除单细胞生物外，所有的动物身上都有某种神经系统。

9. No matter how____, it is not necessarily worthless.

　　A. dry a desert may be　　　　　B. a desert may be dry

　　C. may a desert be dry　　　　　D. a desert dry may be

【分析】该题主要考查让步状语从句，no matter how+ 形容词（副词）+ 正常语序的句子，表示"不管怎样"，故选 A。

【译文】不论一片沙漠多么干燥，它都不一定毫无价值。

10. The Smithsonian Institution preserves more than sixty-five million items of scientific,historical, or artistic interest, ____winning the popular title "attic of the nation".

　　A. however　　　　　　　　B. thus

　　C. and　　　　　　　　　　D. moreover

【分析】该题主要考查原因状语从句，连接副词 thus 表递进，故选 B。

【译文】斯密森学会收藏着多达六千五百万项科学、历史、艺术等物品。因而被人们俗称为"国家的阁楼"。

二、专项练习

（一）语法与词汇选择题

1. Tony was the only one of the students who ____ named Outstanding Student.

　　A. is　　　　　　　　　　　B. are

　　C. was　　　　　　　　　　D. were

2. It is required that the students ____ the term paper tomorrow.

　　A. finished　　　　　　　　B. finish

　　C. will finish　　　　　　　D. may finish

3. Look at John. He is sitting there _____ in deep thought.

    A. being lost   B.lost

    C. losing   D. having lost

4. The workers _____ the subway by next year.

    A. will have built   B. are going to build

    C. will build   D. are building

5. It is necessary to find an engineer _____ has skills that meet your needs.

    A. whom   B. which

    C. whose   D. who

6. This new style of sports shoes is very popular and it is _____ in all sizes.

    A. important   B. active

    C. available   D. famous

7. In his report of the accident he _____ some important details.

    A. missed   B. wasted

    C. escaped   D. failed

8. It is very cold outside, and you should _____ your coat to keep warm.

    A. put on   B. take off

    C. get along   D. carry on

9. He is such a genius that he finished the task _____ within only three months.

    A. completely   B. narrowly

    C. lightly   D. necessarily

10. It will _____ us two years to finish the training program.

    A. cause   B. spend

    C. pay   D. take

11. A good _____ can make a good ending.

    A beginning   B.begin

    C.origin   D.source

12. The key _____ succcss is hard work and persistence.

    A. on   B. for

    C.to   D.of

13. Four people were seriously _____ in an accideut on the motorway.

    A.injured   B. illness

    C.hurt   D.pain

14. He had to ____ his studies because of lack of money.

    A.give away   B.give up

    C.give off   D.give in

15. ____ for a job is a painful experience, but one that nearly everyone must endure at least once in a lifetime.

    A. Finding   B.Hunting

    C.Regarding   D. Reviewing

16. Without proper lessons,you could ____ a lot of bad habits when playing the piano.

    A.warm up   B.pick up

    C.clen up   D.catch up

17. I don't know what his interests are, because we talked ____ about work when we meet.

    A.main   B.mainly

    C.major   D.majorly

18. By ____ Mr. Smith is a bus driver.

    A. employment   B.work

    C.business   D. occupation

19. History was his ____ in the college. He teaches history now.

    A mayor   B.minor

    C.miner   D.major

20. She refused to ____ the door key to the landlady until she got back her deposit.

    A. find   B.lose

    C. forget   D.hand over

21. We tried to ____ him down, but he kept shouting and swearing.

    A.calm   B.quiet

    C.get   D.make

22. The captain ____ an apology to the passengers for the delay caused by bad weather.

    A.make   B. said

    C.put   D. passed

23. Those plastic flowers look so ____ that many people think they are real.

    A.bad   B.natural

    C.comparable   D. similar

24. This is the second ____ of this dictionary.

    A.version   B.publication

    C.editor   D.edition

25. The People's Republic of China was ____ in 1949.

    A.founded   B.constructed

    C.created   D.set up

26. ____ a reply, he decided to write again.

    A. Receiving   B. Receiving not

    C. Not having received   D. Having received

27. After watching ____TV, she played ____ violin for an hour.

    A. /; /   B. the; the

    C.the; /   D/; the

28. All the preparations for the task ____, and we're ready to start.

    A.completes   B.complete

    C .been completed   D.have been completed

29. —Alice, why didn't you come yesterday?

    —I ____ , but I had a unexpected visitor.

    A.hadn't   B.wouldn't

    C.was going to   D.didn't

30. As she ____ the newspaper, Granny ____ asleep.

    A.read, was falling   B.was reading, fell

    C.was reading, was falling   D.read, fell

31. —Can I join your club, Dad?

    —You can when you ____ a bit older.

    A.will have   B.will

    C.getting   D.get

32. —Did you listen to Mr. Jackson's lecture?

    —Yes. I have never heard a ____ one.

    A. more exciting   B. more excited

    C. most exciting   D. most excited

33. How I wish I ____ to my parents' advice.

    A.listening   B.had listened

    C.am listening   D.listen

34. He speaks Chinese as fluently as if he _____ a Chinese.

    A.were   B.been

    C.are   D.has

35. The man spoke at the meeting yesterday _____ his brother.

    A. had been   B. was

    C. has been   D. is

36. You _____ John in the street this morning. He's been dead for ages.

    A. mustn' t see   B. mustn' t have seen

    C. Couldn't see   D. couldn' t have seen

37. The woman went in and told her husband _____ the old men had said.

    A. what   B. who

    C. which   D. that

38. The soldier found him _____ a hero when he returned to his village.

    A. someone of   B. someone

    C. something   D. something of

39. She hired a woman to help her with the housework _____ that she could spend more time with her child.

    A. in   B. such

    C. for   D. so

40. We had to _____ into the ground to find water.

    A. dig deeply   B. dig deep

    C. deeply dig   D. deep dig

41. Yesterday morning, I went to _____ school, which stood in _____ sight of my house to tell him about the terrible accident.

    A. /, the   B. the, /

    C. the, the   D. /, /

42. The vice–president and production director of the company _____ the welcoming ceremony held by the Capital Hill this evening.

    A.is to attend   B.are to attend

    C. were to attend   D. have attended

43. The hospitals were filled with patients, old and young _____ from breath–related problems.

    A. suffered   B. suffers

    C. suffering   D. suffer

44. Only years later ____ the truth about the matter.

    A. I learned   B. did I learn

    C.I did learn   D. had I learned

45. A ____ is helpful in looking for a job, but it doesn' t mean a job.

    A. record   B. grade

    C. certificate   D. debt

46. To be honest with yourself is to ____ yourself.

    A. look at   B. do

    C. refuse   D. respect

47. College students are expected to ____ a second language.

    A. attend   B. adjust

    C. master   D. suppose

48. The driver fell ____ while driving and killed an old man.

    A. sleeping   B. asleep

    C. to sleep   D.a sleep

49. A newborn baby needs ____ care and attention.

    A. constant   B. fluent

    C. amazed   D. pretty

50. Families, ____ those with young children, have learned a lot from the program.

    A. especial   B. particular

    C. especially   D. really

51. His white hair was in sharp ____ to his dark skin.

    A. difference   B. contrast

    C. opposite   D. background

52. He suffered a serious ____ in the car crash(猛撞), and died on the way to hospital.

    A. injury   B. accident

    C. fall   D. attack

53. While I was walking alone down the street, three men came up to me and asked me for ____ to the beach.

    A. directions   B. contents

    C. materials   D. contacts

54. A foreigner's first ____ of the US is likely to be that everyone is in a rush—often under pressure.

    A. effect   B. entry

C. impression   D. addition

55. China has been ____ great importance to the development of its economy all the time.

     A. offering   B. devoting

     C. attaching   D. dressing

56. He looked a little relaxed, ____ the pleasant surroundings had infected him.

     A. unless   B. if

     C. as if   D. even if

57. The reason why she studied hard was ____ she didn't want her parents to feel disappointed.

     A. that   B. because

     C. what   D. whether

58. We should develop healthy eating habits and take exercise regularly to ____ our strength.

     A. take up   B. make uo

     C. build up   D. set up

59. The problem was ____ complicated ____ be explained clearly in just several sentences.

     A. too, to   B. so, too

     C. very, that   D. too, that

60. In my opinion, the birthday cake bought by my mother ____ very easily.

     A. will be cut   B. is cut

     C. cuts   D. to cut

（二）用括号中所给单词的适当形式填空

1. I remember ____（see）her last year at Mary's birthday party.

2. Students would rather try once again than ____（give）up the plan.

3. Greenpeace is an international ____（organize）that works to protect the environment.

4. Scientists have done a lot of study to show that praise is far ____（effective）than criticism in improving students' behaviour.

5. The secretary was in a good mood because her ____（propose）was accepted by the general manager.

6. I hope you keep us ____（inform）of how you are getting along with your work.

7. If I ____（be）you, I would not ask such a silly question.

8 .You should send me the report on the program ____（immediate）.

9. The new flexible working time system will enable an ____（employ）to work more efficiently.

10. There is a well-known proverb: The more haste, the ____（little）speed.

11. Children always ask their parents for ____（person）space.

12. I am afraid we can not afford ____（take）a taxi. Let's go by underground instead.

13. People begin to try their best to reduce air ____（pollute）for the sake of the environment and their health.

14. COVID-19 has been spreading around the globe, ____（cause）over 500,000 deaths.

15. This statement tries to fool you into believing in the ____（assume）that the tooth paste cures bad breath.

16. In November the temperatures drop and the days ____（short）.

17. He said he would come soon but we ____（wait）for half an hour.

18. The drug has a ____（benefit）effect on the immune system.

19. Most of the time I feel ____（energy）even after I have worked for a whole day.

20. There is still room for making ____（improve）.

21. By this summer, we will ____（live）for five years.

22. Wealthy as he is, he is ____（economy）in all areas of his life.

23. He's decided to visit the house and see if it is worth ____（buy）.

24. If I were you, I ____（visit）the company's website for more detailed information.

25. ____（like）his quiet sister, he is active and lively in the eyes of his friends.

26. You might begin to think about someone who was kind, ____（consider）and friendly.

27. Mary ____（do）like surfing the Internet, and she often spends hours online.

28. David talked with a friend of ____（he）on the Internet for a long time yesterday.

29. Having your phone ____（damage）may cause a lot of trouble to you.

30. Because of the snowstorm, many passengers could do nothing but ____（stay）at the airport.

第二节 完形填空

一、例题分析

Computers can't think. They can imitate, pretend and copy. But they can't 1.____the human imagination. No computer could produce a single line of Henry V. Nor could it 2.____one photographic picture or lure one child into an inappropriate relationship.3.____textbooks and teachers,computers give what is asked for, regardless of age or appropriateness, education or ability. Thus, computers require more, 4.____less, teaching.They require parents to accept their children having 5.____to a lot of information.What they do with 6.____depends on how much they know. How much they know depends on 7.____they are taught,at home and at school. A world open to inquiring minds is one fraught with dangers. It is also one 8.____with excitement. Computers mean kids need more, not less information.They need lessons 9____philosophy, morality, critical and creative thinking. None of that comes from a computer. It comes from10.____, schools, churches and a wealth of writing that explores the great questions.

 1. A. help   B. replace   C. take   D. instead

 2. A. produce B. offer   C. describe D. provide

 3. A.Like   B. Unlike   C. As   D. Otherwise

 4. A. or   B. no   C. nor   D. not

 5. A. entrance B. access   C. exit   D. pass

 6. A. it   B. them   C. those   D. him

 7. A. which   B. that   C. what   D. where

 8. A. pleased B. satisfied C. full   D. filled

 9. A. in   B. on   C. for   D. of

 10. A. friends B. classmates C. parents D. teachers

【分析】

1. B 本题为词义辨析题。译文:但是它们不能代替人类的想象力。help,帮助,促进; replace（v.）,代替,取代; take,拿走,携带; instead（adv.）,代替,反而。

2. A 本题为逻辑推理题。根据上文,该处为原词重复。produce,生产,制造; offer, 主动提出,提供（东西或机会等）; describe,描述; provide,提供,供应。

3. B 本题为词义辨析题。译文:与课本和老师不同,计算机提供人们要求的信息,不管年龄大小、合适与否、教育水平或能力高低。like，像……一样；unlike，不像，与……不同；as，如同；otherwise，否则，不然。

4. D 本题为逻辑推理题。根据上文，计算机提供人们要求的信息，不管年龄大小、合适与否、教育水平或能力高低。这里要表达的是：计算机需要更多，而不是更少的指导。

5. B 本题为词语搭配题。have access to, 使用（或见到）……的机会；entrance，入口，进入权；exit，出口，退出；pass，合格，通行证。

6. A 本题为逻辑推理题。译文：孩子们怎么利用计算机取决于他们的了解有多少。根据上文：计算机需要更多指导，这要求父母接受一个事实，即孩子们有使用大量信息的机会，所以此处应用 it 指代上文的 information。

7. C 本题考查句子结构。On 后面是宾语从句，从句成分不完整，缺少宾语。which 在宾语从句中作主语或宾语，有选择的含义；that 在宾语从句中只起连接作用，不充当任何成分；where 在宾语从句中作地点状语。

8. D 本题为词义辨析题。译文：这是一个充满刺激的世界。be pleased with，对……满意；be satisfied with，对……满意；be full of，充满……的；be filled with，充满……。

9. B 本题为词义辨析题。译文：他们需要关于哲学、道德规范、批判性和创造性思维的课程。In，在……内，关于，在……方面；on，关于，lesson on 关于……的课程；of，属于（某人或物）；for，对于，为了。

10. C 本题为逻辑推理题。译文：这些思维方式来自父母、学校、教堂，以及探讨这些问题的大量著作。根据上文：…they are taught, at home and at school，可知此处表示的是来自"父母"。

二、专项练习

（一）

people will probably think that literature（文学）is a form of art that can be enjoyed without formal instruction. However, people with 1.____knowledge of literature may miss a lot when reading a novel, play or essay.

These readers are comparable to the spectators（观众）at a football game who watch the game and enjoy it without really understanding the complex movements 2.____ on the field. Although they may enjoy the game, many spectators watch only the ball generally, missing entirely the contribution of other members 3.____ the total play as well as the intricacies（复杂）happening within the match. A person who understands football — or better yet, has played the game — is more 4.____ of judging when a team is playing well or 5.____ and is also likely to enjoy a "good" game or more. The 6.____ is true of reading literature. Most people have read many literary works, but many do not understand or 7.____ the author's skill in communicating. Just like those spectators of the football game,they can hardly enjoy a "good" book. This book is 8.____ intended to help you learn to 9.____ attention not only to what happens, but to how it happens and how the author has 10.____ it—to analyze literary works so that you can fully experience them.

1. A. many   B.informal   C.several   D.much

2. A. occurred   B. to be occurred   C. having been occurred D. occurring

3. A. at   B. within   C. to   D. about

4. A. able   B. unable   C. possible   D. capable

5. A. succeed   B. success   C. successful   D. successfully

6. A. same   B. such   C. other   D. another

7. A. realize   B. appreciate   C. know   D. recognize

8. A. then   B. therefore   C. so   D. however

9. A. pay   B. call   C. draw   D. focus

10. A. drawn   B. presented   C. maintained   D. explained

（二）

There are many places that are special for me: a tiny beach in Cornwall where we used to 1.____ family vacations during the endless summer holidays; my grandparents' country cottage with its garden 2.____ of wild flowers and bird song; a photo in my geography textbook of a mountain scene 3.____ Switzerland, which I've only ever visited in my daydreams. All of these, places have been special to me in their own way at various times in my life, but there is one place that has always been there for me, a place that I visit every day— my bedroom.

On the surface, my bedroom is pretty much like any 4.____ bedroom. It's got a door, a window and, of course, a bed. It's an unusual color, though: bright red, like the red of a big juicy tomato. I had a huge argument 5.____ my parents about the color. They wanted me to paint it green because it would be good for my 6.____.

I told them red would be good for my imagination. I won and they 7.____ let me paint it myself. That was fun. Of course, another reason I love my bedroom is 8.____ it's where I keep all my things. I generally like to keep them all over the floor and under the bed— something else my parents and I 9.____ disagree over.

What 10.____ can I tell you about my room? There are posters on the wall, usually of pop stars, which tend to get changed every few months. There's a small desk and a chair beneath a window that overlooks the street below. Looking out of the window, I can spend hours watching the world go by while I pretend I'm working. And that's really all there is to say about it. So why do I like it so much? Well, because it's mine. It's a place I can escape to whenever I want.

1. A. take   B. spend   C. set   D. make

2. A. full   B.fill   C, fool   D. feel

3. A. to   B. off   C. on   D.in

4. A. another   B. other   C. others   D. one

5. A. with   B. in   C. on   D. out

6. A. vision   B. concentration   C. station   D. relation

7. A. right   B. anyway   C. even   D. yet

8. A. as   B. because   C. though   D. why

9. A. hardly   B. never   C. ever   D. occasionally

10. A. else   B. other   C. way   D. plus

（三）

No two people act, think, or feel the same way 1.____ makes you unique is mainly a result of heredity（遗传）, family, roles, culture, etc. Heredity is the passing . 2.____ of traits, or characteristics and qualities, from parents to their children. Some of these traits are 3.____ , such as your eye color, your facial features, and your body build. Heredity also can play a part in your intelligence.

Your family is one of the 4.____ influences on the person you are 5____ . Are you an only child, the oldest child, the 6.____ child, or a middle child? What activities do you do with 7.____ members? These questions suggest some of the ways you are 8.____ by your family.

The roles you have determine how you relate 9.____ other people and how you act in various 10.____. A role is your position in a group or situation. You have many roles.

You may be a daughter or a son at home, or a student at school. Your roles vary, depending on the people with whom you interact and the situations involved. You learn your roles by talking to and watching people who are important to you.

1. A. that   B.it   C. which   D. what

2. A. over   B. out   C. on   D. up

3. A. physical   B. mental   C. intellectual   D. emotional

4. A. heaviest   B. strongest   C. slightest   D. weakest

5. A. becoming   B. believing   C. changing   D. belonging

6. A. smallest   B. shortest   C. youngest   D.cleverer

7. A. team   B. group   C.or   D. family

8. A. influenced   B. produced   demanded   D. recommended

9.A. on   B. in   C.to   D. for

10. A. emotions   B. locations   C. situations   D. functions

（四）

Many dog owners who talk to their dogs are convinced that their words are being understood. It 1.____ they may be right. A study at Emory University has found that dogs have a 2.____ understanding of words, are able to distinguish words they have heard before from those they haven't, and are 3.____ to try to understand what is being said to them.

Twelve dogs were 4.____ by their owners to take back two objects based on the objects' names–one soft toy and one rubber toy. The dogs were then 5.____ into an fMRI scanner and had their brain 6.____ monitored while their owners said the names of each toy as they held 7.____ up. As a control, the owner then spoke gibberish words, 8.____ 'bobbu'and 'bodmick', then held up novel objects like a hat or a doll.

They found 9.____ there was more activation in the auditory（听觉的）regions of the dogs' brains when they reacted 10.____ the novel words, suggesting that they sensed that their owners wanted them to understand what they were saying, and were trying to do so.

1. A. turns on   B. turns up   C. turns off   D. turns out

2. A. basic   B. bad   C. clean   D. major

3. A. keen   B. eager   C. interested   D. excited

4. A. trained   B. training   C. treating   D. treated

5. A. placed   B. place   C. placing   D. to place

6. A cooperation   B. contact   C. activity   D. assignment

7. A.it   B. them   C. those   D. the

8. A.so   B. as   C. such   D. such as

9. A. that   B. which   C. what   D.where

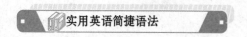

10. A. by   B. with   C.to   D. on

（五）

As children move towards adulthood（成年）, they become taller, stronger, and more independent. At some point in adulthood,1.____, a slow decline begins. Their hair often 2.____ gray, their skin wrinkles, and their muscles begin to 3.____ Their short-term memory may suffer, and they often 4.____ part of their vision or hearing.Scientists are not 5.____ sure what causes the effects of aging. The body might have a time 6.____which would determine how long the cells can remain 7.____. Depending on the type of animal and its environment, animals age at different rates and live 8.____ different lengths of time. An animal in a good zoo—well 9.____and protected from predators（捕食者）— often lives longer than the same type in the wild. 10.____, people who live in rich countries generally live longer than 11.____ in poor countries. Several other factors also 12.____ how long people live and the quality of their lives. One factor is genetics（遗传）.In some families, it seems that many 13.____ have long lives. Genetics may also determine whether people 14.____ certain diseases. Another factor is lifestyle. People who keep their minds 15.____ and often communicate with friends will feel younger and may live longer. People who keep a normal weight, exercise, and do not smoke may also age more slowly.

 1. A. moreover   B. besides   C. therefore   D.however

 2. A. falls   B. turns   C. stays   D. seems

 3. A. grow   B. develop   C. shrink   D. fade

 4. A. lose   B. harm   C. protect   D. improve

 5. A. simply   B. exactly   C. purely   D. strictly

 6. A. label   B. lack   C. link   D. limit

 7. A. healthy   B. bright   C. stable   D. secure

 8. A. with   B. on   C. in   D. for

 9. A. clothed   B. trained   C. behaved   D. fed

10. A. Finally   B. Mostly   C. Commonly   D. similarly

11. A. those   B. that   C. others   D. some

12. A. judge   B. form   C. cause   D. affect

13. A. friends   B. members   C. races   D. names

14. A. take   B. make   C. get   D. cause

15. A. calm   B. clever   C. film   D. active

第三节 阅读理解

一、例题分析

Cattle have served humanity since prehistoric（史前）days as beasts of burden and as supplier of leather, meat, and milk. Some of the earliest written records concern the sale of cattle. These valuable animals are unusual in that they do not have front teeth in their upper jaw. Instead they chew with their back teeth and gums（齿龈）. Cows swallow their food quickly and store it in the fat stomach or rumen, the first of the four compartments in the stomachs. Later the food passed into the second stomach or reticulum where it is rolled into little balls or cuds.While resting ,cows cough up these cuds and chew them more thoroughly.This time the food passes into the third and then the fourth stomach, where digestion takes place. Bacteria in cow's stomach aid in digesting the cellulose in terms of grass or hay.

Over one hundred million head of cattle are raised in the United States. Dairy cattle produce more than fifteen and one-half billion gallons of milk every year. Although dairy cattle are bred primarily to produce milk, about half the beef used in United States comes from dairy breeds. This is because when dry（no longer producing milk）they fatten quickly and produce high-quality beef.

1. Questions: According to the passage, what is the rumen?

A. The first stomach compartment.

B. The name of the upper jaw.

C. The stomach where digestion（消化）takes place.

D. The name of the bacteria（细菌）in the cow's stomach.

【解析】本题为细节理解题，根据第一段 Cows swallow their food quickly and store it in the fat stomach or rumen, the first of the four compartments stomachs in their.. and 和 or 并列前后内容意义相近，所以 rumen 与 stomach（胃）意思相近，再根据下面的 firs.... 可知选 A。

2. The cow's second stomach is used primarily for_____.

A. food storage

B. the production of milk

C. digestion

D. the creation of cuds

【解析】本题为细节理解题，由原文中"Later the food passed into the second stomach or reticulum where it is rolled into little balls or cuds. "之后，食物通过第二道胃，在这里食物被卷成球体或者反刍，所以牛的第二道胃是将食物卷为球体或者进行反刍，故选 D。

3. Which of the following is essential in the digestion of the cellulose in the cows stomach?

    A. Cud   B. Reticulum

    C. Bacteria   D. Grass

【解析】细节理解题，由原文中 "Bacteria in cow's stomach aid in digesting the cellulose in terms of grass or hay." 题目问以下哪些在奶牛胃中纤维素的消化中是必需的？牛胃中的细菌有助于消化草或干草中的纤维素。故选 C。

4. Which of the following statements about cows is NOT true?

    A. Cows are suppliers of leather, meat and milk

    B. Cows chew and digest their food quickly

    C. Cows cough up cuds to chew them more thoroughly

    D. Cows produce high-quality beef when dry

【解析】下面关于奶牛的哪一种说法是不正确的？奶牛会快速地咀嚼和消化它们的食物，文章未提到很快，故选 B。

5. What does the passage say about the beef consumed in the United States?

    A. Half of it comes from cows that beef consumed in the United States?

    B. Much of it contains a lot of fat

    C. Half of it comes from dairy breeds

    D. Much of it is of poor quality

【解析】本题为细节理解题，根据 "in the United States" 定位到 "about half the beef used in United States comes from dairy breeds." 这段话关于美国牛肉的消费说明了什么？在美国使用的牛肉中，大约有一半来自乳制品。故选 C。

二、专项练习

（一）

Finding a new job is not an easy thing to do. However, our economy is getting stronger, so now might be a good time to start looking. If you think you have the skills and abilities that employers need, there are some things you should do to prepare for the job hunt. First, don't quit your current job until you are sure you have a new one lined up. The best time to look for a job is when you are currently employed. People who are unemployed and desperate（极度渴望的）for work sometimes make bad decisions in accepting a job offer. Consider job offers carefully.

Will the new job be better than the one you are having now? What about the location? Will the commute to work be easy or difficult? If a person doesn't have good English skills, it'simportant to work on fixing that as soon as possible. It takes the average person five years to learn English really well, but for people who have lived in our country for a few years already, it might take a little less time than that. Many cities offer free English classes through the public schools, or you can learn English online. You can take classes at night or on the weekend. Good English skills usually make it easier to find a job and move up to better positions within a company.

1. The writer believes that now might be the right time for job hunting because of ____.

    A. the rising economy

    B. the increasing export

    C. the high consumption

    D. the substantial investment

2. You are advised not to give up your present job ____.

    A. until you have got a pay rise

    B. before you are sure to get a new one

    C. unless your boss asks you to leave

    D. because you may lose a chance for promotion

3. According to the passage, what might happen to unemployed people who are desperate for work?

    A. They may find a dream job.

    B. They may lose their benefits.

    C. They might make a poor decision.

    D. They might end up working in another city.

4. What advice does the author offer if a person's English skills are not good enough?

    A. Looking for a private tutor.

    B. Improving them as soon as possible.

    C. Moving to an English speaking country.

    D. Practicing their English with a native speaker.

5. One advantage of having good English skills is that ____.

    A. it helps you to get promotion

    B. it helps you to learn new techniques

    C. it enables you to fit in a new environment

    D. it enables you to get along with your colleagues

（二）

Why don't birds get lost on their long flights from one place to another? Scientists have puzzled over this question for many years. Now they're beginning to fill in the blanks.

Not long ago, experiments showed that birds rely on the sun to guide them during daylight hours.But what about birds that fly at night? Tests with artificial stars have proved that certain night-flying birds are able to follow the stars in their long-distance flights.

A dove had spent its lifetime in a cage and had never flown under a natural sky.Yet it showed an inborn ability to use the stars for guidance. The bird's cage was placed under an artificial star-filled sky. The bird tried to fly in the same direction as that taken by his outdoor cousins. Any change in the position of the artificial stars caused a change in the direction of his flights.

But the stars are apparently their principal means of navigation. When the stars are hidden by clouds, they apparently find their way by such landmarks as mountain ranges, coast lines, and river courses. But when it's too dark to see these, the doves circle helplessly, unable to find their way.

6. Why do not birds get lost on long flights?

A. Reasons are known by everyone.

B. Reasons probably remain a mystery.

C. Scientists have recently discovered reasons.

D. Scientists haven't yet discovered reasons.

7. How do birds avoid getting lost in the daytime?

A. They use the sun for guidance.   B. They rely on landmarks.

C. They fly by GPS.   D. They fly aimlessly.

8. What does "his outdoor cousins" in Paragraph 3 refer to?

A. Doves under the natural sky.   B. Birds in general.

C. Other experimenters.   D. Artificial stars.

9. The experiment with the dove shows that_____.

A. birds can not fly long distances

B. birds can fly only by following the herd

C. birds are taught to navigate

D. some birds seem to follow the stars for guidance

10. In total darkness, doves_____.

A. don't know how to find their way　　B. fly back home

C. wait for stars to appear　　D. use landmarks

（三）

The food we eat seems to have effects on our health. Although science has made enormous steps in making food more fit to eat, it has, at the same time, made many foods unfit to eat. Some research has shown that perhaps 80% of cancers are related to the diet as well. Different cultures are more prone to contract certain illness because of the food that is characteristic in these cultures. That food related to illness is not a new discovery. In 1945, government researchers realized that nitrates（硝酸盐）and nitrites（亚硝酸盐）, commonly used to preserve color in meat, and other food additives, caused cancer. Yet, these carcinogenic additives（致癌的添加剂）remain in our food, and it becomes more difficult all the time to know which things on the packaging labels of processed food are helpful or harmful.

The additives which we eat are not all so direct. Farmers often give penicillin（青霉素）to beef and poultry, and because of this, penicillin has been found in the milk of treated cows. Sometimes similar drugs are administered to animals not for medical purposes, but for financial reasons.

The farmers are simply trying to fatten the animals in order to obtain a higher price of the market. Although the Food and Drug Administration（食品药品管理局）has tried repeatedly to control these procedures, the practices continue.

11. Which of the following would be the best title for the passage?

　　A. Food and Illness　　B. Food and Culture

　　C. Food and Science　　D. Food and Health

12. Nitrates and nitrites can be used for.

　　A. processing food　　B. preserving color in meat

　　C. packaging　　D. treating cows

13. Which of the following statements is NOT correct?

　　A. The food we eat has no effect on our health.

　　B. That food related to illness is not a new discovery.

　　C. Sometimes drugs are given to animals for financial reasons.

　　D. We eat some of the food additives directly and indirectly.

14. Why do farmers give drugs to their animals?

A. To make the animals' meat fit to eat.

B. To make the animals' meat rich in nutrients.

C. To make the animals fatter.

D. To make animals' meat healthy.

15. We can learn from the passage that.

A. 90% of cancers are related to the diet

B. some additives are harmful to our health

C. scientists have made all the food fit to eat

D. carcinogenic additives can not be found in processed food

（四）

Tom brought his report card home in the afternoon. He didn't want to show it to his parents. He put it under the bed. Then he threw his schoolbag on the table and went into the sitting room and turned on the TV. There was a football game on it and he began to watch it. But after supper his dog Bobby went under the bed and brought his report card out. His mother saw it and began to read.

"Oh, dear!" the woman called out, "You are not good at all. Look! You get a zero in the English test, and in the math test, too. Oh! You pass only P.E. Tell me how you study at school."

"Don't be angry, Mom," said Tom. "Nobody is perfect, you know!"

16. Tom went home ____ .

A. in the morning   B. in the afternoon

C. at noon   D. at night

17. Tom is good at ____ .

A. English   B. math

C. all his lessons   D. P.E

18. Tom put his report card under the bed because ____ .

A. he hoped to look after it   B. he was afraid that his parents may see it

C. it was too big   D.it was no use

19. Who is Bobby?

A. Tom's mother.   B. Tom's father,

C. Tom's brother.   D. Tom's dog.

20. The woman was angry because ____ .

A. her son put his report card under the bed

B. the dog found the report card

C. her son was not good at his lessons

D. her son liked football at school

（五）

Fiona was popular at school. She was clever and humorous. She was kind and friendly to everyone. She invited all her classmates to her birthday party, and sometimes she gave presents to her friends. She was a busy girl so she never spent time with only one friend.

Everything changed on National Friendship Day. On that day, everyone got three presents and gave them to their three best friends. Fiona bought presents for three of her friends. But when all the students gave their presents to each other, Fiona was the only one who didn't get a present! She felt terrible, and spent hours crying. Why?

When she came home at night, she asked her mother for advice. "My dear, you're a nice girl," said her mother, "but you can't be a close friend to everybody. You don't have enough time to be with all of them. So everyone can only have a few true friends." Hearing this, Fiona changed her way. At last, she had some true friends.

21. What was Fiona like according to the passage?

    A Humorous and friendly.　　　　　　B. Kind and unfriendly.

    C. Clever but unfriendly.　　　　　　D. Friendly but not clever.

22. The underlined word "terrible" in Paragraph 2 means "____" in Chinese.

    A. 幸运的　　　　　　　　　　　　B. 极坏的

    C. 愉快的　　　　　　　　　　　　D. 骄傲的

23. Why did Fiona feel terrible according to the passage?

    A. Because she had no friends at school.

    B. Because no one wanted to play with her.

    C. Because she didn't have money to buy presents.

    D. Because she didn't get a present on National Friendship Day,

24. Which of the following is TRUE according to the passage?

    A. Fiona never spent time with only one friend.

    B. Fiona didn't buy presents on National Friendship Day.

    C. Fiona had fun on National Friendship Day.

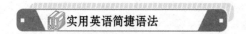

D. Fiona didn't have any true friends at last.

25. What's the best title for the passage?

A. How to Make Many Friends   B. How to Buy Presents

C. Make True Friends   D. Enjoy Yourself

（六）

Is advertising really necessary? Billions of dollars are spent on it every year, so it must be important. After all, it's a busy world. You have to advertise to get people's attention to sell products!

Not every company thinks that way, however. Despite avoiding traditional ways of advertising, the NO-AD company ("no-ad" stands for "not advertised") has seen a steady increase in their profits over the years. And because their advertising plan is atypical they can save money and keep costs down. That makes their products more affordable for consumers.

NO-AD sells its products by word of mouth, "Word-of mouth advertising" happens when one person tells another about a good experience with a product or service. That second person then tells another friend, family member, or colleague. And so a chain of information is created.

Typically, advertisers talk about how good their product is. Although they say things like, "Studies show that our product is the best," or "Everyone loves this product," it can sound insincere or unconvincing. It's much more believable to hear about a product from a family member or friend who has used it and liked it. Our loved ones' opinions are very important to us, so we often listen to their advice about a product.

Word-of-mouth advertising has other advantages, too. It's cost-effective (after all, It's free) and a company doesn't have to create a complex business plan to do it. Here is some advice for small businesses about word-of-mouth advertising:

Be prepared to talk about your company at any time. You never know who you will meet.Always carry business cards.

Only say positive things about your company. Don't say negative things about your competitors.

Help other companies by referring people to them. The more you help others, the more good fortune will come back to you, and that's good business!

26. Why do companies spend money to advertise?

A. Because they want to sell their products.

B. Because they want to compete with others.

C. Because they want to call people's attention.

D. Because they want to compare prices with others.

27. What does the underlined word "atypical" mean in the passage?

    A. Reasonable   B. Regular

    C. Acceptable   D. unusual

28. In what way does NO-AD sell its products?

    A. word-of-mouth   B. word-of-TV

    C. word-of-media   D. word-of-company

29. Why is NO-AD method successful to a certain degree?

    A. Because we love products.

    B. Because we trust our loved ones' words.

    C. Because they show the best products.

    D. Because the products are believable.

30. What is the most important for small business about word-of-mouth advertising?

    A. Always carry business cards with you,

    B. Be ready to sell your products any time.

    C. Helping others means helping yourself.

    D. Always say bad things about your competitors.

（七）

Scientists find that hard-working people live longer than average men and women. Career women are healthier than housewives. Evidence shows that the jobless are in poorer health than jobholders. An investigation shows that whenever unemployment rate increases by 1%, the death rate increases correspondingly by 2%. All this comes down to one point: work is helpful to health.

Why is work good for health? It is because work keeps people busy away from loneliness. Researches show that people feel unhappy, worried and lonely when they have nothing to do. Instead, the happiest are those who are busy.

Many high achievements who love their careers feel that they are happiest when they are working hard. Work serves as a bridge between man and reality. By work people come into with each other. By collective activity they find friendship and warmth. This is helpful to health.

The loss of work means the loss of everything. It affects man spiritually and makes him ill. Besides, work gives one a sense of fulfillment and a sense of achievement. Work makes one feel his value and status in society. When a writer finishes his writing or a doctor successfully operates on a patient or a teacher sees his students grow, they are happy beyond words.

From the above we can come to the conclusion that the more you work the happier and healthier you will be. Let us work hard and study and live a happy and healthy life.

31. The underlined word "average" in Paragraph 1 means____.

    A. healthy   B. lazy

    C. ordinary   D. poor

32. The reason why housewives are not as healthy as career women is that____.

    A. housewives are poorer than career women

    B. housewives eat less food than career women

    C. housewives have more children than career women

    D. housewives have less chance to communicate with others

33. Which of the following statements is TRUE according to Paragraph 2?

    A. Busy people have nothing to do at home.

    B. There is no friendship and warmth at home.

    C. High achievers don't care about their families.

    D. A satisfying job helps people to keep one healthy.

34. If a doctor successfully operates on a patient, he could feel____.

    A. very satisfied   B. very unhappy

    C. very tired   D. very heady

35. The best title for this passage may be____.

    A. People Should Find a Job

    B. Working is Good for Health

    C. People Should Make More Friends by Work

    D. The Loss of Work Means the Loss of Everything

（八）

For many women choosing whether to work or not to work outside their home is a luxury. They must work to survive. Others face a hard decision. Perhaps the easiest choice has to do with economics. One husband said, "Marge and I decided after careful consideration that for her to go back to work at this moment was an extravagance we couldn' t afford. "With two preschool children, it soon became clear in their figuring that with babysitters, transportation, and increased taxes, rather than having more money, they might actually end up with less.

Economic factors are usually the first to be considered, but they are not the most important. The most important aspects of the decision have to do with the emotional needs of each member of the family. It is in this area that husbands and wives find themselves having to face many confusing and conflicting feelings.

There are many women who find that homemaking is boring or who feel imprisoned if they have to stay home with a young child or several children. On the other hand, there are women who think that homemaking gives them the deepest satisfaction.

From my own experience, I would like to suggest that sometimes the decision to go back to work is made in too much haste. There are few decisions that I now regret more. I wasn' t mature enough to see how much I could have gained at home. I regret my impatience to get on with my career. I wish I had allowed myself the luxury of watching the world through my little girl's eyes.

36. Why do many women have to work outside their home?

    A. Because their economic situation decides that they have no other alternative.

    B. Because they don't like looking after the children at home.

    C. Because doing the housework is very dull and unpaid.

    D. Because they think the work outside their home is a luxury for them.

37. Why did Marge and her husband consider it an extravagance for Marge to go back to work?

    A. Because they might pay more than they earned on the whole.

    B. Because Marge has to take care of their children at home.

    C. Because they don't have a baby sister to help them..

    D. Because Marge has to pay more transportation fares.

38. What are the two major considerations in deciding whether women should go out to work?

    A. The economic factor and their social status in life.

    B. The social status and the family role they play in the family.

    C. The economic factor and the emotional needs of family members.

    D. Requirements of the society.

39. Some women would rather do housework and take care of their children than pursue a career because they feel____.

    A. highly stressed while working at home

    B. greatly competitive at work

    C. surprisingly upset while working with men

    D. deeply satisfied with their work at home

40. If given a second chance, the author would probably choose to ____ .

    A. work outside home and make a lot of money

    B. stay at home and take care of her family

    C. work outside home one week and stay at home the other

    D. observe the world in their little daughter's eyes

（九）

We use both words and gestures to express our feelings, but the problem is that these words and gestures can be understood in different ways.

It is true that a smile means the same thing in any language. So does laughter or crying. There are also a number of striking similarities in the way different animals show the same feelings. Dogs, tigers and humans, for example, often show their teeth when they are angry. This is probably because they are born with those behavior patterns.

Fear is another emotion that is shown in much the same way all over the world. In Chinese and English literature, a phrase like "he went pale and began to tremble" suggests that the man is either very afraid or he has just got a very big: shocked. However, "he opened his eyes wide" is used to suggest anger in Chinese whereas in English it means surprise. In Chinese "surprise" can be described in a phrase like " they stretched out their tongues" . Sticking out your tongue in English is an insulting gesture or expresses strong dislike.

Even in the same culture, people differ in ability to understand and express feelings. Experiments in America have shown that women are usually better than men at recognizing fear, anger, love and happiness on people s faces. Other studies show that older people usually find it easier to recognize or understand body language than younger people do.

41. According to the passage, ____.

    A. we can hardly understand what people's gestures mean.

B. we cannot often be sure what people mean when they describe their feelings in words or gestures.

C. words can be better understood by older people

D. gestures can be better understood by most of the people while words can not

42. People's facial expressions may be misunderstood because _____.

A. people of different ages may have different understandings

B. people have different cultures

C. people of different sexes may understand a gesture in different way

D. people of different countries speak different languages

43. Even in the same culture, people _____.

A. have different abilities to understand and express feelings

B. have exactly the same understanding of something

C. never fail to understand each other

D. are equally intelligent

44. From this passage, we can conclude _____.

A. words are used as frequently as gestures

B. words are often found difficult to understand

C. words and gestures are both used in expressing feelings

D. gestures are more efficiently used than words

45. The best title for this passage be _____.

A. Words and Feelings

B. Words, Gestures and Feelings

C. Gestures and Feelings

D. Culture and Understanding

（十）

The air is polluted. The earth is poisoned. Water is unsafe to drink and rubbish is burying the civilization that produced it.

Our environment is being contaminated faster than nature and man's present efforts can prevent it. Time is bringing us more people, and more people will bring us more industry. More people and more industry will bring us more motor vehicles, larger cities, and the growing use of man-made materials. This is happening not only in advanced societies but among the developing nations as they become industrialized. Pollution is, in a sense, exported.

Now many scientists are expressing fears about the possibility of world pollution. Some experts declare that the balance of nature is being so upset that the very survival of humanity is in danger.

What can explain and solve this growing problem? The fact is that pollution is caused by man – by his greed and his modern way of life. We make increasing "industrialization" our chief aim. For its sake we are willing to sacrifice everything: clean air, pure water, good food, our health and the future of our children. There is a constant flow of people from the countryside into the cities, eager for the benefits of our modern society. But as our technological achievements have grown in the last twenty years, so in that time pollution has become a serious problem. The connection is clear.

Isn't it time we stopped to ask ourselves where we are going and why? It reminds one of the stories about the airline pilot who told his passengers over the loudspeaker, "I've some good news and some bad news. The good news is that we're making rapid progress at 530 miles per hour. The bad news is that we're lost and don't know where we're going." The sad fact is that this becomes a true story when applied to our modern society.

46. What does the word "contaminated" the first sentence of the second paragraph mean according to passage ?

    A. Contained   B. Consumed

    C. Examined   D. Polluted

47. Which of the following sentences is not true according to the author?

    A. The author wants to tell us that pollution is a serious problem caused by man.

    B. We can stop this trend of pollution merely by our own efforts.

    C. Many scientists show their worry about the world pollution.

    D. The pollution of the earth will threaten the human being's survival.

48. Who caused this problem according to the passage?

    A. The motor cycles.   B. The growing industries

    C. The human beings.   D. The larger cities.

49. Why do people constantly move from the countryside into the cities?

    A. Because the earth in the countryside was polluted.

    B. Because there are more jobs provided in the cities

    C. Because it is easier to make a living in the cities.

    D. Because they are eager to get the benefits of modern cities.

50. What is the author's purpose by concluding his article with a story?

A. To show that though we have made great progress in development we lost our direction in the modern society.

B. To illustrate that we are now in the process of flying a plane with a confused pilot driving it.

C. To prove that neither flying a lost plane nor directing the way of a plane is an easy job.

D. To make sure that everybody is the cause of our world pollution through everybody's making rapid progress.

 第四节　翻译

一、例题分析

1. It is hard to imagine what would happen in the world if there were no electricity now.

　　A. 你能猜到，没有电的时代，人们是怎样生活的吗？

　　B. 难以想象世界上如果没有电，生活会是什么样子。

　　C. 很难想象如果现在没有电，世界会出现什么情况。

　　D. 你猜猜看，如果现在不用电，世界还会是这样吗？

【分析】该句包含一个 what 引导的宾语从句和一个 if 引导的非真实条件句，对现在的情况进行假设。宾语从句可采用顺译，条件状语从句则一般先译从句部分。It is hard to imagine，译为：很难想象；if there were no electricity now，译为：如果现在没有电；what would happen in the world，世界会出现什么情况。故选 C。

2. Sunlight is no less necessary than fresh air to a healthy condition of body.

　　A. 日光和新鲜空气对于身体健康是不可缺少的。

　　B. 为了健康的身体，日光和新鲜空气一样不可缺少。

　　C. 由于身体健康，日光如同新鲜空气一样不可或缺。

　　D. 阳光同新鲜空气一样对于身体的健康不可缺少。

【分析】该句是简单句，含有一个 no less…than… 的比较级结构。sunlight 意为：阳光，日光；no less necessary than fresh air 译为：与新鲜空气一样不可缺少；a healthy condition of body 译为：身体的健康。故选 D。

3. Seen from the tower at night, the theme park looks even more magnificent with all its lights on.

【分析】该句含有一个过去分词短语，作条件状语。Seen from the tower 译为：从塔上望过去；more magnificent 译为：更加壮丽；with all its lights on 译为：所有灯亮起来，表示状态。故选 B。

二、专项练习

（一）选择题

1. Compared with the developed countries, some African countries are left far behind in terms of people's living standard. （　　）

    A. 与发达国家相比，一些非洲国家在人民生活水平上还相差甚远。

    B. 相比发展过的国家，一些非洲国家的人民生活水平远远落后。

    C. 与发达国家相比，在人民生活水平方面一些国家在非洲很落后。

    D. 与发展完善的国家比起来，非洲国家的一些人民生活水平很落后。

2. No matter how long or short the letter is, what really counts is that it is heart-warming. （　　）

    A. 信的长短无所谓，真正可以计数的是它能温暖人心。

    B. 写信的时间长短无所谓，真正可以计数的是它能温暖人心。

    C. 不管信是长还是短，真正重要的是它能温暖人心。

    D. 写信的时间长短无所谓，关键是它能温暖人心。

3. No one can use cellphones in any areas at the hospital where equipment might be affected by the interference from cell phones. （　　）

    A. 在医院的任何区域都不得使用手机，因为会受到设备的干扰。

    B. 在医院的部分区域，手机会影响设备的使用，任何人都不得使用。

    C. 医院里没有人使用手机，因此不会影响设备的使用。

    D. 医院内，在可能干扰设备使用的任何区域，禁止使用手机。

4. Jiuzhaigou is noted for its varieties of exotic plants and flowers, rare birds and animals. （　　）

    A. 九寨沟上有一告示，爱护奇花异草、珍奇鸟兽。

    B. 九寨沟以奇花异草、珍奇鸟兽而著名。

    C. 进入九寨沟要注意，不要破坏奇花异草、珍奇鸟兽。

    D. 九寨沟以奇花异草而闻名，但少有珍奇鸟兽。

5. He grows flowers as well as vegetables. （　　）

    A. 他种花不种菜。

    B. 他不种花种菜。

C. 他种花和种菜一样好。

D. 他既种菜也种花。

6. To know what is good and to do what is right is not the same thing. （　）

A. 知道好和实际做是不同的。

B. 知道什么是好的，和做什么是对的，是不同的。

C. 知道好不好，和做得好不好，是不一样的。

D. 知道做什么，和做得对不对，是不一样的。

7. People have realized the importance of a healthy diet to their health. （　）

A. 人们已经认识到健康饮食的重要性。

B. 人们已经将健康饮食对健康的重要性落到实处。

C. 人们已经承认健康饮食的重要性。

D. 人们已经认识到引进健康饮食方式的重要性。

8. A lot of people have helped you. Don't let them down. （　）

A. 许多人帮助过你。不要让他们失望。

B. 许多人要帮助你。不要让他们失望。

C. 许多人打算帮助你。不要让他们失望。

D. 许多人帮助过你。不要让他们下去。

9. Mary returned, saw the mess, and hit the roof. （　）

A. 玛丽回来了，看到了一片狼藉，撞上了屋顶。

B. 玛丽回来了，看到了一片狼箱，掀了屋顶。

C. 玛丽回来了，看到了一片狼箱，大发雷霆。

D. 玛丽回来了，看到了一片狼藉，打掉了屋顶。

10. Our outstanding personnel have driven our success and established us as a world class leader in the computer industry. （　）

A. 我们的专业技术人员成功地开发了一款新的软件，为我们行业的发展作出了贡献。

B. 我们的优秀雇员使得我们在计算机行业取得成功，并且推动了计算机技术的发展。

C. 我们的杰出人才促进了我们的成功，确立了我们在计算机行业的世界级领导地位。

D. 我们的优秀人才促使了我们的成功，在计算机领域做出了贡献。

11. We employ over 100,000 employees nationwide, whose goal is to deliver the highest level of service and improve the customer experience. （　）

A. 我们在全国聘用了 10 多万员工，他们的目标是提供最高水平的服务并改善客户体验。

B. 我们公司的员工积极参加业务培训，10 几万员工中有许多人都获得了专业技术的证书。

  C. 我们的 10 多万员工分布在全国各地，他们尽了自己最大的努力向客户提供优质产品。

  D. 我们雇用了 10 多万员工，分布在全国各地，目标是提供优质产品。

12. Effective business communication helps build a good relationship between the employer and the staff, which can help increase productivity and the company's bottom line.（　）

  A. 和谐的雇主和员工之间的关系取决于他们之间的及时交流，这可以有效地帮助公司提高生产力。

  B. 有效的业务沟通有助于在雇主和员工之间建立良好的关系，这能帮助提高生产力和公司的赢利。

  C. 良好的企业文化能够促进公司员工之间的相互谅解和尊重，这有利于公司提高自身的市场形象。

  D. 有效的商业关系有助于在雇主和员工之间建立友好的关系，进而提高公司的竞争力。

13. In recent decades, environmental problems have been on the rise as the result of human activities and unplanned management of the technological development.（　）

  A. 近几十年来，人类活动的范围不断延伸，导致全球气候变暖的问题日益严重。

  B. 近几十年来，日益变坏的环境问题与人类从事的活动和科技进步息息相关。

  C. 近几十年来，由于人类活动和技术开发的无计划管理，环境问题一直在增加。

  D. 近几十年来，环境一直在恶化，由于人类活动的结果和技术开发的无序管理。

14. This matter is so important that it should not be left in the hand of inexperienced lawyers.（　）

  A. 如此重要的事情，没有经验的律师不敢接手。

  B. 这件事事关重大，不能交给缺乏经验的律师来处理。

  C. 这件事也很重要，不应让有经验的律师处理。

  D. 这样重要的事情，没有经验的律师是不敢接手的。

15. No matter how hard I tried to explain how to operate the machine, they were still at a loss.（　）

  A. 尽管我努力把机器开动了，他们还是觉得非常失望。

  B. 无论我怎么努力地说明机器的用法，他们都不理解我。

  C. 即使我努力地对机器做了解释，他们还是不相信我的话。

  D. 不管我怎么努力地解释如何操作这台机器，他们依然听不懂。

16. We accept returns or exchanges within 30 days from the date of the purchase of these cellphones.（　）

A. 手机从购买之日起 30 天内我们接受退换。

B. 手机在试用 30 天之后我们可允许退货。

C. 我们同意 30 天内可以购买手机，退货或更换。

D. 我们保证 30 天内购买的手机，包退包换。

17. Good managers can create an environment in which different opinions are value and everyone works together for a common goal. （　　）

　　A. 大家一定要齐心协力地工作，创造一个良好的环境，发表各种不同看法。要做好经理。

　　B. 为了共同的目标，好经理应该尊重各种不同意思，与大家一起工作，创造良好的氛围。

　　C. 好经理能够创造一种氛围，让不同意见受到尊重并且每个人都有为共同目标合作奋斗。

　　D. 为了共同的目标，好经理应该能够提出各种宝贵的意见，为大家创造良好的工作氛围。

18. If either party wants to renew the contract, it should submit a written notice to the other party three months prior to the expiration of the contract. （　　）

　　A. 如果任何一方希望撤销合约，必须将撤销的理由在三个月内通知对方。

　　B. 如果合同一方希望重签合同，必须在合同到期三个月内写信通知对方。

　　C. 如果任何一方希望更改合同，必须提前三个月向对方书面提交其理由。

　　D. 如果合同一方希望续签合同，必须在合同期满前三个月书面通知对方。

19. There is no sign that the world economic crisis will lesson in the next few month, although a certain degree of recovery is in sight. （　　）

　　A. 尽管没有人认为未来几个月内世界经济危机会消失，但是在一定程度上的复苏是肯定的。

　　B. 尽管世界经济复苏的迹象是肯定的，但是未来几个月内经济危机缓和的现象还不很明显。

　　C. 尽管已经显现出一定程度的经济复苏，但没有迹象表明，世界经济危机在未来几个月会减缓。

　　D. 尽管没有人承认未来几个月内世界经济危机会触底，但我们肯定会看到世界经济的复苏。

20. Most of the issues concerning personnel management have been solved satisfactorily. Only a few of secondary importance remain to be discussed. （　　）

　　A. 多数有关人员管理的问题顺利地解决了，仅剩下几个问题还需要进行第二次讨论。

　　B. 多数有关人事管理问题已经得到圆满解决，仅剩下几个次要问题还有待于讨论。

C. 很多有关人员配备问题基本上都得到了答复，只有第二个重要问题还未经过讨论。

D. 第二个重要问题是有关人员调动的问题，这次已经得到妥善解决，不必再次讨论。

（二）段落翻译

1. Youth is not a matter of time but a matter of self-improvement, both physically and morally. Being a good youth, one should have the basic factor-health. A healthy body is a kind of priceless treasure, and one can do nothing without it. Secondly, we should value our moral character. We should be always willing to help those in trouble without any complaints. Thirdly, cooperation and communication also play an important role in being a good youth. Nobody can work out every problem without help of friends or partners. So being a good youth really needs to take every effort to make yourself perfect.

2. When you get into a car accident, there is something you can do to make sure that everyone is safe. You should first check yourself for injuries. If you are injured, call 120 or ask someone else to do so. If you are seriously injured, try not to move, and wait for emergency personnel. If you're not too hurt to move, check on the other passengers in your car. If anyone is injured, get on the phone with emergency services.

3. If you want to get a driver's license, you will have to apply at a driver's license office. There you will be required to take a written test for driving in that area. You will also need to pass an eye test. If you need glasses, make sure you wear them. In addition, you must pass an actual driving test. If you fail the written or driving tests, you can take them again on another date.

4. Pollution is a problem because man in an increasingly populated and industrialized world is upsetting the environment in which he lives. The growing population makes increasing demands on the world's fixed supply of air, water and land. This rise in population is also accompanied by the desire of more and more people for a better standard of living. But the problem of waste material to be disposed of has been causing concern to living things and their environment.

5. Difficulties arise in the lives of us all. What is most important is dealing with the hard times, dealing with the change, and getting through to the other side where the sun is still shining just for you. It takes a strong person to deal with tough times and difficult choices. It takes courage. It takes being an active participant in our life. Hang in there and take care to see that we don't lose sight of the one thing that is constant, beautiful, and true. Everything will be fine.

6. Nowadays a large number of universities encourage and organize students to take

part in social practice activities. During the holidays, more and more students choose to be volunteers, take part-time jobs, or take part in other activities alike. Undoubtedly, students have benefited a lot from social practice activities. First, they are provided with more opportunities to know the real world outside the campus. What's more, in social practice activities, students can apply their theoretical knowledge to the solution to the practical problems. So their practical skills are improved greatly. Besides, social practice activities help strengthen students' sense of social responsibility.

附录 1 常见短语

a large number of	大量的
a little	少量，一点
a sort of	一种
above all	首先
add up to	合计达
add up	总计，加起来
after a while	过了一会
after all	毕竟
again and again	反复地，再三地
ahead of	提前
all but	几乎
all in all	总而言之
all of a sudden	突然地
all over	到处
all right	好
all sorts of	各种各样的
all the same	仍然
all the time	一直，始终
and so on/forth	等等
anything but	绝非，决不
as/so long as	只要
as a matter of fact	实际上
as a result of	由于，作为……的结果
as a result	结果
as a rule	通常
as a whole	作为整体

as far as	直到……为止，只要……
as follows	如下
as for/to	关于
as if/though	好像
as soon as	一……就……
as well as	除……之外（也），此外
as well	也，同样
aside from	除……之外
ask for	请求
at a loss	不知所措
at a time	每次，曾经
at all costs	不惜任何代价
at all	根本
at any price	不惜任何代价，无论如何
at any time	随时
at best	至多，顶多
at first	起初，首先
at hand	在手边，在附近
at least	起码，至少
at length	最后，详细地
at most	至多
at no time	从不，决不
at once	立即
at one time	曾经
at present	目前
at the cost of	以……为代价
at the end of	在……结尾
at the foot of	在……脚下
at the latest	最迟，最晚
at the moment	此刻
at the price of	付出……的代价
at the same time	同时
back and forth	来回地
be dressed in	穿……
be fed up with	对……厌烦

be known to	为……所知
be late for	迟到
be mad at sb./sth.	对某人（某物）恼火
be made from	由……制成（看不出原材料）
be made of	由……制成（看出原材料）
be made up of	由……组成
be open to	开放
be rich in	富含……
be short of	缺乏
be sure of	对……有把握，确信
be sure to do	确定／一定会做……
be tired of	对……感到厌烦
be tired with/from	因……而疲劳
be wild to do	渴望做……
be wild with	因……而发狂
be worth doing	值得做……
because of	因为
before long	不久以后
beyond belief	难以置信
beyond control	无法控制
beyond doubt	无疑地
beyond expression	无法表达
bit by bit	一点一点地
blow up	爆炸，暴怒
book store	书店
break down	垮掉，分解
break in	闯入，打断
break into	破门而入，侵占
break off	中断，突然停止
break out	爆发
break the law	违法
break the rule	违反规则
break through	突破
bring about	导致，引起
bring forth	产生，提出

bring out	公布，出版
bring through	使安全度过
bring up	养育
bring/carry/put into effect	实施
build on	把……建立于
build up	逐步建立，增强
bus stop	车站
but for	若非，要不是
by all means	无论如何
by and large	大体上，总的来说
by chance	偶然
by far	到目前为止，最
by hand	用手
by means of	通过……方式
by mistake	错误地
by nature	生来
by no means	决不
by now	到如今
by reason of	由于
by the way	顺便地
call at	拜访，访问
call back	回电话
call for	要求
call in	召集
call on	号召
can not help doing	禁不住做某事
care about	担心
care for	关怀
carry on	继续开展，随身携带
carry out	执行
catch a cold	感冒
catch fire	着火
catch hold of	抓住
catch one's breath	喘息，屏息
catch one's eyes	引起某人的注意

catch sight of	瞥见
catch up with sb./sth.	赶上某人／某物
catch up	赶上
change one's mind	改变主意
check in	登记，报道
check out	结账离开
clean up	打扫干净
clear away	把……清除掉
come about	发生
come across	偶遇
come down	下来，退步
come from	来自
come on	快点
come out	出现，出版
come over	过来
come round	恢复知觉，苏醒，到来
come through	经历
come to an end	结束
come to one's sense	苏醒过来
come to the point	说到要点
come to	达到，苏醒
come true	实现
come up to	达到
come up with	提出
come up	上升，升起；发生；被提及
common sense	常识
count in	把……计算在内
count on	依靠，指望
cover up	掩盖
cut across	抄近路通过
cut down	砍倒
cut in	插入
cut off	切断
cut short	缩减
date back to	追溯到……

date from	起源
die down	渐渐消失
die of	死于……
die out	灭绝
differ from	不同于
differ with	和……意见不一致
do away with	废除，去掉
do good to	有益于
draw out	抽出，取出
draw up	草拟，起草
dream of	梦想，渴望
dress up	精心打扮
drop by/in	顺便拜访
drop off	离开，减弱
drop out	不参与，退学
eat up	吃光
end up	结束
even so	虽然，即使
even if/though	虽然如此
every other	每隔一个的
except for	除……之外
face up to	勇敢地面对
fail to do	未能……
fall apart	崩溃
fall asleep	睡着
fall behind	落后
fall ill	生病
fall in love	坠入爱河
fall into	陷于
far away	遥远
far from	远非，离……远
feed on	以……为食
feel like	想要做某事，摸上去像……
fight against	对抗
fight for	为……而战

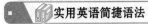

续表

find fault with	挑……的毛病
first of all	首先
for a moment	一会儿
for a while	暂时，一会儿
for all	尽管
for fear of/that	担心，以免
for free	免费
for good	永久地，一劳永逸地
for nothing	免费地；徒然地
for short	缩写
for sure	当然，一定，毫无疑问
for the first time	第一次
for the moment	目前，暂时
for the time being	暂时
from now on	从现在开始
from time to time	有时，不时
from top to bottom	彻底地，从上至下的
get across	越过，通过；使了解
get along with	与……相处
get away	离开，逃脱
get by	通过，过得去
get down	下来，下车
get hold of	抓住
get in touch with	与……取得联系
get into trouble	遇到困难
get into	进入，陷入
get in	进入，到达，收获
get off	下来，出发，逃脱惩罚
get on with	继续做……
get on	登上
get out	出去
get over	克服，熬过
get ready for	为……做好准备
get rid of	摆脱，除去
get through	通过

get to know	变得熟悉，逐渐了解
get together	相聚
get up	起床
give away	赠送，分发；泄露
give in	屈服，让步
give off	散发
give out	分发，用完
give up	放弃
give way to	让步，让位于……
go about	着手
go after	追逐，追求
go against	反对，违反
go ahead	前进
go away	离开
go bad	变质，变坏
go down	下降
go on with	继续
go out	出去，熄灭
go over	温习
go through	通过
go with	和……相配
go wrong	出问题
hand down	传下来
hand in hand	手拉手
hand in	上交
hand out	分发
hand over	移交
hang on/up	不挂断 / 挂断（电话）
have nothing to to with	和……无关
have something to do with	和……有关
head for	前往
hear about	听说（知道而已）
hear of	听说（非常了解）
heart and soul	全心全意地
hold back	踌躇

hold on to	坚持
hold one's breath	屏住呼吸
hold out	伸出，坚持
hold up	支持，延迟，举起
hurry up	快点
in a hurry	匆忙地
in a sense	在某种意义上
in a short while	过一会儿，不久
in a way	在某种程度上
in a word	简言之
in all	总共
in any case	无论如何
in case of	假设
in case	万一，如果
in common	共同的，共用的
in doubt	怀疑的
in danger	在危险中
in effect	实际上
in front of	在……前面
in nature	本质上
in need of	需要
in no case	决不
in no time	马上
in no way	决不
in other words	换句话说
in person	亲自
in place of	代替
in place	合适
in public	公开地
in question	被讨论的
in return for	作为对……的报答
in return	作为报答，作为回报
in short	总而言之
in store	储藏，准备着
in surprise	惊奇地

续表

in that	在于，因为
in the course of	在……期间
in the end	最后
in the face of	面对着
in the first place	首先
in the long run	从长远来看
in the middle of	在……中间
in the name of	以……的名义
in the open air	在户外
in the open	在露天
in the presence of sb.	在……面前
in the same way	同样
in time	及时
in trouble	处于困境
in turn	依次，轮流
in view of	鉴于，由于，考虑到
join in	参加
just as well	没关系，那样也好
keep an eye on	照看
keep back	阻止
keep in mind	牢记
keep in touch with	与……保持联系
keep off	让开，远离
keep on （doing sth.）	继续（做某事）
keep one's word	守信用
keep to	遵循，坚持
keep up with	跟上
keep up	保持
kind of	有点儿，有几分
knock at	敲
knock into	撞上
later on	稍后，后来
lay down	放下，规定
lay out	布置
lead to	导致

续表

lean on	靠着
least of all	尤其不，最不
leave behind	留下
let alone	不管
let go	释放，松开
little by little	渐渐地
live on/off	靠……生活
live through	经历过
live up to	实践，做到，不辜负
long for	渴望
look after	照顾
look around	环顾四周
look at	看
look back	回顾
look down on/upon	看不起
look forward to	期望
look for	寻找
look into	调查
look on	旁观
look out	留神，当心
look over	调查，检查
look round	到处寻找
look through	浏览
look up	抬头看，查找
lose heart	丧失勇气
lose sight of	看不到
lose weight	减肥
make a face	做鬼脸
make for	犯错误
make friends	有利于……
make fun of	取笑
make one's way	前进，往前
make out	辨认出，听懂
make room for	为……腾出空位
make sense of	搞清……的意思

make sense	有意义
make sure	查明，确保
make the best/most of	充分利用
make up for	弥补
make up one's mind	下决心
make up	化妆，编造
make use of	利用
mean doing	意味着
mean to do	打算做
meet with	偶遇
mistake…for	误认为，当作
mix up	混淆，弄混
more and more	越来越多
more or less	或多或少
move away	离开
move on	继续前进
move out	搬出
name after	根据……命名
next to	仅次于
no doubt	怪不得
no longer	不再
no more than	只是
no more	不再
no sooner than	一……就
nothing but	只有，只不过
now and then	偶尔
now that	既然
on business	因公
on duty	值班
on earth	到底，究竟，在世上
on end	连续地
on fire	着火
on foot	步行
on one's part	就某人而言
on purpose	故意地

续表

on show	展出
on the air	在广播中
on the other hand	另一方面
on the whole	总的来说，大体上
on time	准时
on top of	在……的上面
once again	再一次
once in a while	偶尔；间或
once more	再一次
once upon a time	从前
one after another	一个接一个，相继
open up	展开，开放
or else	否则
or so	大约
other than	除了
out of breath	喘不过气来
out of control	失去控制
out of date	过时的
out of danger	远离危险
out of question	毫无疑问
out of the question	不可能
out of work	失业
owing to	由于
pay a visit to	拜访
pay back	偿还，汇报
pay for	支付
pay off	还清
pick out	挑选
pick up	捡起
play a part in	对……有影响
play the role of	扮演……的角色；起……作用
play with	与……一起玩
point of view	看法，观点
point out	指出
point to	指向

续表

pull down	摧毁
pull in	进站，到岸
pull up	减速停下
put aside	放到一边
put away	收起来，放好，储存
put down	拒绝，放下，镇压
put forward	提出
put off	推迟
put on	张贴
put out	伸出，熄灭
put up with	容忍
put up	举起，提高，张贴
put……to use	使用
quite a few	相当多的
reach an conclusion	得出结论
regard……as	把……看作
regret doing sth.	后悔做过某事
regret to do sth.	遗憾去做某事
remember doing	记得做过某事
remember to do	记住要去做某事
result from	起因于
result in	导致
rib sb. of sth.	使某人摆脱某物
right away	立刻
rule out	排除在外
run into	撞上，陷入
run off	逃跑
run out of	用完
run over	碾过，溢出
run short of	缺少
run through	跑着穿过
save up	储蓄，贮存
see sb. off	给某人送行
see through	看穿
see to（it that）	务必

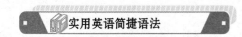

续表

send for	派人去请
send in	递送，送来
send out	发送
set about	着手工作
set aside	搁置
set back	使……延迟，阻碍
set down	记下
set forth	出发
set free	释放
set off	启程
set out	着手
set up	搭建
shout at	朝……大嚷
shout to	朝……大声喊话
show off	炫耀
show sb. around	带某人四周转转
show up	露面
side by side	并肩
slow down	慢下来
so as to	如此……以至于
so far	迄今为止
so that	如此……以至于
sooner or later	迟早
sort out	挑选出
speak of	提起
speak out	说出
spend…in doing sth.	花费（时间、金钱）做……
spend…on sth.	花费（时间、金钱等）在……上
stand for	代表，象征
stand out	突出，显眼
stand up to	勇敢地面对，经得起
stand up	站起来
start out	动身，开始
start with	首先，一开始
step by step	逐步地

step up	提高，加快
stop doing	停止做……
stop from	阻止
stop to do	停下来去做……
struggle against	同……作斗争
struggle for	为……而斗争
struggle to do sth.	努力，尽力做某事
such as	例如，诸如
such that	如此……（以致）
take a chance	冒险
take a look at	看
take after	与……相像
take along	随身带着
take as	把……作为
take away	清除，拿走
take care of	照顾
take care	当心
take delight in	以……为乐
take down	写下，记下
take effect	生效
take in	理解
take off	脱下，起飞
take on	承担，从事
take over	接着，接替
take part in	参与
take place	发生
take steps（to do sth.）	采取行动
take the lead	带头，居首位
take turns	轮流
take up	占去，开始从事
take…by surprise	使……吃惊
talk of	谈论，议论
talk over	商议，议论
talk to/with	与某人谈论
tell…from	把……和……区分开

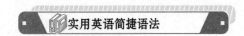

the other day	前几天
the same as	和……一样
think about	思考
think of…as	把……看作是
think of	想起，认为
think over	仔细考虑
throw away	扔掉
to be honest	坦率地说
to one's surprise	令人吃惊的是
to one's taste	合……的口味
to the point	中肯
together with	和……一起，连同
try one's best	竭尽全力
try on	试穿
try out	试验
turn a blind eye to	对……视而不见
turn down	调低，拒绝
turn into	把……变成
turn off	关掉
turn on	打开
turn out	结果是……
turn to	求助于……
turn up	调高，出现
under control	在掌握之中
up and down	上下地，来来往往
up to date	最新的
up to	从事于，达到，取决于
use up	用光
view…as	把……看作
wake up	唤醒
warn sb. against doing	警告某人不要做……
warn sb. of/about sth.	警告某人注意……
wash out	洗净，冲掉
wash up	洗（盘、碗、手、脸）
watch for	等待，留心

续表

watch out for	密切注意，戒备
watch over	查看，监视
what about	……怎么样
what if	如果……将会怎样
what's more	更重要的是
win over	把……争取过来
with/in regard to	关于
with/for the purpose of	为了
word for word	逐字地
work on	继续工作，从事
work out	想出，制定出，算出
worry about	担心，烦恼
write down	记下，写下

附录 2 双语热词（二十大报告）

新征程	new journey
中国式现代化	Chinese path to modernization
第二个百年奋斗目标	the second Centenary Goal
江山就是人民	This country is its people.
人民就是江山	The people are the country.
人民至上	put the people first
团结奋斗	strive in unity
中华民族伟大复兴	the great rejuvenation of the Chinese nation
踔厉奋发、勇毅前行	forge ahead with enterprise and fortitude
谦虚谨慎、艰苦奋斗	stay modest, prudent, and hardworking
新发展理念	new development philosophy
全过程人民民主	whole-process people's democracy
脱贫攻坚	eradicate absolute poverty
一带一路	Belt and Road Initiative
社会公平正义	social fairness and justice
总体国家安全观	a holistic approach to national security
平安中国	Peaceful China Initiative
人类命运共同体	a human community with a shared future
全面从严治党	full and rigorous Party self-governance
历史周期律	historical cycle
共同富裕	common prosperity for all
人与自然和谐共生	harmony between humanity and nature

两步走	two-step strategic plan
乡村振兴	rural revitalization
人才强国战略	workforce development strategy
创新驱动发展战略	the innovation-driven development strategy
全面依法治国	law-based governance on all fronts
中国故事	China's stories
健康中国	Healthy China Initiative
美丽中国	Beautiful China Initiative
永远吹冲锋号	keep sounding the bugle
零容忍	zero tolerance
人民首创精神	the pioneering spirit of our people
高质量发展	high-quality development
新发展格局	a new pattern of development
战略性举措	strategic measures
变革性实践	transformative practices
标志性成果	landmark advances
撸起袖子加油干	roll up our sleeves and got down to work
加强改革顶层设计	enhance top-level design for reform
创造性转化、创新性发展	creative transformation and development
以人民为中心的发展思想	a people-centered philosophy of development
中国特色大国外交	Major-country diplomacy with Chinese characteristics
治国理政新理念新思想新战略	new ideas, new thinking, and new strategies on national governance
不忘初心、牢记使命	never forget our original aspiration and founding mission
全面建成小康社会	finish building a moderately prosperous society in all respects
马克思主义中国化时代化	adapt Marxism to the Chinese context and the needs of our times
中国共产党的中心任务	the central task of the Communist Party of China
全面建成社会主义现代化强国	build China into a great modern socialist country in all respects
中国人的饭碗牢牢端在自己手中	China's food supply remains firmly in its own hands

续表

科教兴国战略	strategy for invigoration China through science and education
反腐败斗争攻坚战持久战	the tough and protracted battle against corruption
中国特色社会主义伟大旗帜	the great banner of socialism with Chinese characteristics
人类和平与发展崇高事业	the noble cause of peace and development for humanity

附录 3 参考答案

第一章

第一节 名词

一、用所给单词的适当形式填空

1. glasses   2. light   3. women   4. else's   5. Alice mother's

6. student   7. minutes'   8. Germans   9. brothers-in-law 10. Bamboos

11. lives   12. centuries 13. brother's 14. yesterday's 15. Furniture

二、单项选择题

1-5 DDABA   6-10 DDBCD

11-15 CBBBB   16-20 BADCD

21-25 DBCCB   26-30 CCDCA

第二节 代词

一、用所给单词的适当形式填空

1. yours   2. yourself   3. them   4. his   5. ours

6. I   7. theirs   8. hers   9. Its   10. them

二、单项选择题

1-5 DDDBD   6-10 BADBD

11-15 ACCAB   16-20 ACBAA

21-25 BBABB   26-30 DBACB

第三节 冠词

一、用 a, an, the 或 / 填空

1. a   2. a   3. /, the   4. an   5. The

6. the, /   7. /   8. /   9. /   10. the

11. the   12. an, /   13. the   14. /, the   15. a, the

二、单项选择题

1–5 AADDB   6–10 CBDDC

11–15 DBCDC   16–20 AACBD

21–25 ABBBD   26–30 DADDB

第四节　数词

一、用所给单词的适当形式填空

1. twelfth   2. third   3. thousands   4. ninth   5. seven

6. fourth   7. hundred   8. twenty–first   9. second   10.first

二、单项选择题

1–5 DBBDC   6–10 BDBCA

11–15 CBBAC   16–20 CBBAB

21–25 BADBA   26–30 AABCC

第五节　介词

一、用适当的介词填空

1. on   2. at   3. until   4. since   5. by

6. on   7. on   8. for   9. at   10. in

11. since   12. at   13. in   14. on   15. at

16. in   17. with   18. in   19. with   20. by

21. by   22. at   23. on   24. except for   25. besides

26. by   27. from   28. as   29. on   30. on

二、单项选择题

1–5 DDCBA   6–10 BABCA

11–15 BCBAA   16–20 DCBAD

21–25 BBCBC   26–30 DACDB

31–35 DCBCA   36–40 BDAAB

第六节　形容词和副词

一、用所给单词的适当形式填空

1. earlier   2. the wettest   3. farther, farthest   4. wealthy

5. elder, older　　　6. best　　　　　7. tallest　　　　　8. longest

9. the most comfortable　　　10. strong

二、单项选择题

1–5 BDBCB　　　　6–10 DDBBC

11–15 DDDDD　　　16–20 BBBCC

21–25 DCCBB　　　26–30 ACBCA

第七节　动词和动词短语

一、用所给单词的适当形式填空

1. healthier　　2. silent　　3. nice　　4. asleep　　5. hungry

6. sadly, sad　　7. stronger　　8. easy, easily　　9. quickly　　10. easily

二、单项选择题

1–5 BBBBB　　　　6–10 BCBAC

11–15 BAADA　　　16–20 DCADA

21–25 DDABD

第八节　情态动词

1–5 CACDA　　　　6–10 CBBDB

11–15 ABDBB　　　16–20 BCADC

21–25 DDCDC　　　26–30 CDBCC

第九节　动词的时态

一、写出下列句子的时态

1. 一般过去时　　2. 现在完成时　　3. 一般现在时　　4. 一般现在时，现在进行时

5. 现在完成时　　6. 现在进行时　　7. 一般过去时　　8. 现在完成时

9. 一般现在时　　10. 一般过去时　　11. 现在完成时　　12. 一般过去时

二、用动词的适当形式填空

1. put　　2. are getting　　3. took, to finish　　4. do

5. is singing　　6. were　　7. has taught　　8. wanted, get

9. has visited　　10. writes　　11. will be　　12. have known

13. comes　　14. will have　　15. has gone　　16. happened

17. is showing　　18. are having, go watch　　19. have, stayed　　20. Have, found

三、用 "never, ever, already, just, yet, for, since" 填空

1. never   2. already   3. for   4. ever, never   5. yet, just

四、单项选择题

1-5 BDDBD	6-10 DBAAB
11-15 DBABC	16-20 BBABB
21-25 ADBBA	26-30 ACAAB
31-35 DDDCC	36-40 BBDCA
41-45 DCDCC	46-50 DBBBD

第十节　动词的语态

一、用所给单词的适当形式填空

1. turned	2. was made	3. be handed
4. will be put	5. cleaning	6. sells
7. were written	8. broke	9. will be held
10. was cut	11. fit	12. will be built
13. was reported	14. last	15. cut

二、单项选择题

1-5 BDBCB	6-10 BDCBC
11-15 BACBA	16-20 CCADB
21-25 CBBBC	26-30 CDABB

第十一节　动词的语气

1-5 BDDBA	6-10 DCBBC
11-15 BBADC	16-20 BCBBD

第十二节　非谓语动词

1-5 ACDCB	6-10 BDBDC
11-15 CBBCC	16-20 CCBCB
21-25 ABCDC	26-30 AABDD
31-35 DACCB	36-40 ACBBD
41-45 BBDAA	46-50 BBCDD

第二章

第一节 简单句和并列句

1–5 ADABC	6–10 CCCCB
11–15 BBBCA	16–20 DDBAA
21–25 CABCA	26–30 ACAAA
31–35 ABABB	

第二节 名词性从句

| 1–5 DCCAB | 6–10 DDDDC |
| 11–15 DCBCB | 16–20 CBABB |

第三节 定语从句

1–5 CBABB	6–10 CAAAD
11–15 ACACB	16–20 CCDBC
21–25 AAACB	26–30 DABBB
31–35 CBDBA	36–40 AAADB

第四节 状语从句

1–5 DBADB	6–10 DABBD
11–15 AACCB	16–20 DDCDA
21–25 DAACD	26–30 BBDAC
31–35 ABBCA	

第五节 主谓一致

1–5 BCCCA	6–10 BBACB
11–15 CBDBD	16–20 BABBB
21–25 CDDDC	26–30 ABBAB

第六节 特殊句式

| 1–5 CBBCB | 6–10 BABAB |
| 11–15 BCBCD | 16–20 DABCB |

第三章

第一节　词汇与语法运用

（一）语法与词汇选择题

1–5 CBBAD	6–10 CAAAD
11–15 ACADB	16–20 BBDDD
21–25 AABAA	26–30 CDDCB
31–35 DABAD	36–40 DADDB
41–45 BACBC	46–50 DCBAC
51–55 BAACC	56–60 CACAB

（二）用括号中所给单词的适当形式填空

1. seeing	2. give	3. organization
4. more effective	5. proposal	6. informed
7. were	8. immediately	9. employee
10. less	11. personal	12. to take
13. pollution	14. causing	15. assumption
16. shorten	17. have waited	18. beneficial
19. energetic	20. improvement	21. have lived
22. economical	23. buying	24. would visit
25. Unlike	26. considerate	27. does
28. his	29. damaged	30. stay

第二节　完形填空

（一）1–5　BDCDD	6–10 ABBAB
（二）1–5　BADBA	6–10 BCBDA
（三）1–5　DCABA	6–10 CDACC
（四）1–5　DABA A	6–10 CADAC
（五）1–5　DBCAB	6–10 DADDD
11–15 ADBCD	

第三节　阅读理解

1–5 ABCBA	6–10 CAADA
11–15 DDACB	16–20 BDBDC
21–25 ABDAC	26–30 ADABC

31–35 CDDAB　　　36–40 AACDB

41–45 BBACB　　　46–50 DBCDA

第四节　翻译

选择题：

1–5 ACDBD　　　6–10 DAACC

11–15 ABCBD　　　16–20 ACDCA

段落翻译：

1. 青春不是时间的问题，而是在身体和道德上自我完善的问题。作为一个优秀的青年，一个人应该有一个基本的因素——健康。健康的身体是一种无价之宝，没有它一个人什么也做不了。其次，我们应该重视我们的道德品质。我们应该总是毫无怨言地乐于帮助那些有困难的人。第三，合作和交流在成为一个好青年中也扮演着重要的角色。没有朋友或伙伴的帮助，没有人能解决所有的问题。所以，成为一个好的年轻人真的需要尽一切努力让自己完美。

2. 当你遇到车祸时，你可以采取一些措施来确保每个人的安全。首先你要检查自己是否受伤。如果你受伤了，请呼叫 120 或叫其他人拨打 120。如果你受了重伤，尽量不要移动，等待急救人员。如果你没有受重伤，还可以动，查看车上其他乘客怎么样。如果有人受伤，请拨打急救服务电话。

3. 如果你想获得机动车驾驶证，你必须到驾照管理办公室申请。你需要在那里参加该地区的驾驶笔试，还需要通过视力测试。如果你需要眼镜，请务必戴着眼镜。此外，你必须通过实际驾驶测试。如果你没有通过笔试或者实际驾驶测试，你可以择日再考。

4. 污染已成为问题，因为在当今人口越来越聚居、社会越来越工业化的世界上，人类正在破坏他们居住的环境。与日俱增的人口导致对世界上有限的空气、水和土地的需求不断增长。伴随着人口的增长，越来越多的人渴望更好的生活水准。但是对于需处理的废弃物问题已经引起人们对生物及其环境的日益关注。

5. 在我们所有人的生活中，困难在所难免。最重要的是挺过艰难的时刻，应对种种变故，到达阳光依然为你山药的彼岸。只有坚强的人才能应对艰难的时刻，作出艰难的选择。这需要勇气。我们需要积极参与自己的人生。坚持下去，当心不要忽视了那永恒的、美好的、真实的事物。一切都将美好。

6. 现在很多大学鼓励并组织学生参加社会实践活动。在假期，越来越多的学生选择去做志愿者、兼职或参加其他类似活动。毫无疑问，学生从社会实践活动中受益匪浅。首先，他们有更多机会了解校园之外的真实世界。更重要的是，在社会实践活动中，他们能把自己的理论知识应用于解决实际问题上，因此他们的实践技能可以得到很大提高。此外，社会实践活动也有助于增强学生的社会责任感。